God's Blueprint
A Complete Study in First John

God's Blueprint

A Complete Study in First John

Michael R Hicks

PUBLISHING

Christian Literature & Artwork

A BOLD TRUTH Publication

God's Blueprint
Copyright © 2020 by Michael R. Hicks
ISBN 13: 978-1-949993-24-0

FIRST EDITION

BOLD TRUTH PUBLISHING
(Christian Literature & Artwork)
606 West 41st, Ste. 4
Sand Springs, Oklahoma 74063
www.BoldTruthPublishing.com ▪ *beirep@yahoo.com*

Available from Amazon.com and other retail outlets. Orders by U.S. trade bookstores and wholesalers. Quantity sales special discounts are available on quantity purchases by corporations, associations, and others. For details, contact the publisher at the address above.

Cover art & overall book design by Aaron Jones.

Printed in the USA.
02 20   10 9 8 7 6 5 4 3 2 1

We would like to recognize and thank these Publishers, for publishing and distributing the following versions of God's written Word.

Dedication

For

God the Father

God the Son

And God the Holy Spirit

Contents

Contents

Contents

Endorsements

"This is a clear and easy to understand commentary designed for the practical application of God's Word."

Deacon Michael Norton
Total Christian Life Ministry
Christian Education Dept.

←■→

"Michael Hicks simplifys Scripture text in ways few have done. He explains difficult text into easy digestible fragmants for the new believer, but enhances the strong meatiness for those believers of full age. No matter what your calling or election, you will be blessed by this gift to the Body of Christ!"

Pastor Steven Conley
Shofar Shepherd's Fold
International Ministries

←■→

"It has been a pleasure to be able to have Michael Hicks as a part of my life for many years now. He is a true man of God. The struggles that he has gone through have brought him to a place where he turns to his God in every situation. His spiritual life guides his every decision. His writing is a gift from God. It comes from a life of prayer and deep study. I have always loved how he backs up the message he shares in his books with countless scriptures. It is easy to see the working of the Holy Spirit on the printed page."

Rev. Duane G. Baker
Pastor and former Prison Chaplain

← ■ →

"It has been a blessing in knowing Michael for approximately fifteen years. It has been awesome to watch him grow spiritually and in wisdom of God's Word. His dedication to the Lord is an inspiration to me as well as to others. Michael's in-depth definitions and insights verse-by-verse, is simple to understand for application, and is truly the leading by the Holy Spirit. He has proven to show his time is studying and research for sharing the knowledge he has gained."

Steve Young
Evangelist, Author, Teacher
Doors of Compassion Ministries
Victory Bible College Sponsor & Distributor
Sapulpa, Oklahoma

← ■ →

"I have known Pastor Michael Ray Hicks for over twenty years now. He has a heart for God inside church and out. His teachings are thorough and informative and I enjoy his delivery of the Word very much. Minister Mike has been living in Christ since I met him in the nineties and I know he has a genuine love for God in his heart. My brother Mike has a unique way of breaking down the Scriptures so those who are not versed can understand spiritually God's intent in his messages. Pastor Mike also shares his experiences with Christ to help others understand exactly what God expects of His children and it's been a pleasure ministering with him."

Terrence Jones
Deacon
Shepherds Fold International Ministries
Del City, Oklahoma

←　■　→

"Pastor Hicks is a man of God and a great Teacher. We've worked together in the ministry for years and it's amazing how he breaks down the Scriptures and makes it plain. Pastor Mike is a compassionate person that always makes the time to help those in need. I'm impressed with him because he has the zeal to teach one or two people as well as a room full. Pastor Mike has been a real blessing in my life."

Starsky Daniels
Minister of Music
YAHJireh Ministries
Oklahoma City, Oklahoma

"The wisdom of Michael Hicks has done it again! A total indepth breakdown and account of this book could not have been explained with more precision and extraordinary fashion. A must read, not only those seeking revelation and a closer encounter with Jesus, but also the Bible scholar looking to increase his knowledge. Well done Sir, continue being an inspiration to the Body of Christ."

Darrell D. Cross
Songwriter

Introduction

In eternity pass, there was an archangel whose body was made of musical instruments such as trumpets, harps, lutes, tumbrels, flutes, and cymbals and so on. It was this angel that led all the other angels in praise and worship to the One who sat on the throne. Since we can't measure time in eternity, there's no way anyone could tell how long Lucifer's swelling pride grew as he attempted to exalt his position. First, it was a thought for God's power, then he coveted God's Throne, and these thoughts surged through him when he directed praise and worship before His Throne. He wanted all the angels praising him in his excellence, so he thought. Then his imagination spurred him on and he said in his heart: "I will ascend into the heavens, I will exalt my throne above the stars, (angels), of God, I will also sit on the mount of the congregations of the farthest side of the north; I will ascend the heights of the clouds, I will be like the Most High."

God knows the hearts of devils and men and wasn't surprised at all with the foolishness of Lucifer. God punished Lucifer for his attempted hostile takeover by breaking him down from a beautiful archangel clothed with musical instruments to Satan enwrapped with evil. The third of the stars that rebelled with him are actually angels and were also reduced to devils and demons. From splendor, magnificence, majesty, and grandeur, they were demoted to defiled, tainted, sullied, and despoiled spiritual beings. These angels were downgraded, demoted, and reduced and they permanently lost their positions in Heaven and received new positions as patrons in the Lake of Fire.

They found out the hard way that you cannot beat God in any way; you can't defeat him, trick Him, overcome Him, or conquer Him. Trying to overwhelm God was/is fruitless and perfectly impossible. Since Satan and his rebel gang of angels couldn't defeat God, they turned their attention to the men and women made in His image upon the earth, God's creation, God's love, God's heart and joy. The devil took it upon himself to personally destroy everyone made in the image of God.

God is our Father, our Creator and can eventually be our friend. He blesses His children with His love, His protection, and His instructions in order for us to live a moral, ethical, honest, decent, and honorable life. He calls us to wisdom, so that we may apply it to the truth. The Bible gives principles which teach us how to live wisely and to please God. After all, our main purpose in life is to please Him. God through wisdom teaches us certain wise practices that we should adhere to, and The Holy Spirit trains us to practice wisdom as a discipline which will lead to the fullness of life.

Introduction

So throughout every generation, demons have been assigned to men and woman to encourage them to be disobedient to God, to rebel against God, and even curse God. These evil entities stir hatred against others. But little did Satan know, God had a plan, and he had no clue about God's plan or what God was about to do.

First, He made Abraham the Father of many nations and established his bloodline for the Christ five thousand years later. Abraham, the first patriarch is the founder of faith and God found favor in him. He believed God no matter what, even to the point of sacrificing his son. God told Abraham his descendants would be like the sand on the beach, and the stars in the sky—too many to count. But the most important thing was Abraham's bloodline, DNA, would be instrumental to host the Savior of the world.

Then *the law* was established, the Ten Commandments through Moses was to show Israel and later, Christians, and the people of the world what He expects from their behavior and lifestyle. Some received it and some did not. So God set the stage for us to be useful through *the Ten Commandments*. These commandments were designed to be a guide to holy and healthy living. When we live by it, we will prosper in every way, when we don't then our worth falters to next to nothing.

Introduction

God said, *"You shall have no other gods before Me."* God demands loyalty and will not share His glory with any other. Israel was surrounded by many different nations who worshipped other gods, and since no human could adequately or sufficiently represent God; He forbade creating any images of Him. Even though God is the Ultimate True and Living God, the devil still influenced men and women to make gods out stone and clay and the materials of the earth to worship the creation instead of the Creator. This is Satan's attempt to get back at God.

God said, *"You shall not take the name of the Lord your God in vain."* The Name of the Lord should not be misused for His Name and his character is inseparable. Through the millennium the Evil One has taken His holy Name and deduced it to a smear amidst the citizens of the world, mixed with cursing and unholy communication and evil living. The Name of God has been misused in magic, in substantiating truth through the use of false oaths, pledges, and promise in blasphemous declarations, remarks and speech. His Name is even shouted out in the midst of sexual intercourse. Taking the Lord's name in vain will carry serious consequences.

God said, *"Remember the Sabbath Day and keep it Holy."* The Sabbath to the world is the opposite of what is holy. There is no day of rest because there are few who set aside a day to rest. Chores need to be done, sports need to be watched, lawns need to be tended, and cars need to be waxed and so on. The Sabbath is supposed to be a day off work but it has become like every other day; drudgery.

God said, *"Honor your father and your mother that your days may be long the in land in which I am giving you."* To *honor* is to prize highly and show respect, to glorify and exalt. Many do not honor their parents any longer; and there are many children who disrespect their parents, by stealing from them, and putting them away in nursing homes just to be done with them, or just neglecting their basic needs in their old age. Then there are those who beat and abuse their parents and even kill them without any remorse, regret, or sorrow. People wonder why death comes early in the lives of some, why they can't live out their full expectancy.

God said, *"You shall not murder!"* Murder is an intentional, wanton, motiveless, or meaningless taking of someone's life. This is not speaking of unintentional, accidental killing but a premeditated act of taking of someone's life. There are 44 murders committed every day. There are murders for hire, murders for fun, murders for revenge, murders for elevation, murders for power, murders for love, murders for sport, murders by the state and country, murders for offense, and murders for hatred, and murders just because. There's a good chance you could be murdered for any reason at any time.

God said, ***"You shall not commit adultery."*** Committing adultery is any form of unfaithfulness. One of the most common acts of adultery is having sexual intercourse outside of marriage or with a married person, someone's wife or husband. You can also commit adultery against God by serving and worshipping created things, like other gods, your money, your house, your car, your job or anything that takes precedence over the worship of God. Today there are billions of false gods wanting to be the All Mighty. These gods covet the worship of men and women and do so by evangelizing those who don't know who they are or don't care about the True and Living God.

God said, "You shall not steal." To steal is to take something that belongs to someone else, illegally without permission, consent, or authorization. Everyone on the planet has stolen something that has belonged to someone else at one time or another. There are those who are sneak thieves while others rob banks. It doesn't matter if you take a little or a lot, a thief is a thief and there is no heaven for thieves.

Introduction

God said, ***"You shall not bear false witness."*** To bear false witness is lie about the truth on any given subject. One of the most common examples is not being truthful in a judicial setting. There are a lot of people who have lied in open court about a situation. Some have spent dozens of years behind prison bars, or lost jobs, or lost spouses because of someone bearing false witness against them. All liars will not make it into Heaven and false witnesses are liars.

God said, ***"You shall not covet your neighbor's house."*** To covet is to desire, lust, or crave for someone's property. It is not the wanting something that is wrong, but wanting it at the expense of others or from a motive of jealously or envy. Coveting and stealing have a lot in common. When a person generally covets a prize, a woman, a car, a house, or a man, they will try to obtain the subject by any means necessary. It is unhealthy to covet anything.

Then God spoke to different Prophets in the span of thousands of years about the activities of the life of Christ. He declared where Christ would be born. He declared His mother would be a virgin. He declared how babies would be killed from the fear of Herod because of the information a baby king just as Pharaoh killed all three old year boys in fear of newborn deliverer. God shared with His Prophets the ministry of Je-

7

sus that He would teach the Gospel, heal the sick, raise the dead, but most importantly, that He would save the world from its sin with the offer of life after death.

Thousands of years later, when the stench of the sins of the world had reached the heavens and the fullness of time had come, God the Father looked over to God the Son and said, "It is time." Jesus then stripped Himself of His eternal power and became an embryo of flesh in womb or the Virgin Mary. None months later, there was a heavenly block party, a celebration of the birth of Jesus the Christ. The Savior of the world came to *break the chains* of bondage, to free all who were spiritually imprisoned, for all who believed in Him.

When the fullness of time came again, Jesus was baptized by John the Baptist for righteousness sake, and when the Holy Ghost came upon Him, God introduced Him as His Son to the world. Then Jesus began to operate with God's blueprint in saying what God says and doing what God does. It was God working through Jesus teaching the Gospel, healing the sick and raising the dead. Every last miracle Jesus did was through the power of God.

Before Jesus was tried, crucified, gave up His Spirit and was raised from the dead, He visited His disciples. He encouraged them and gave them the blue-print for God's plan just as God gave Him the plan of salvation. Fifty days later, the Holy Spirit came as promised and the church was born. Thousands gave their lives to Christ and miracles were happening on a daily basis. The body of Christ grew as the disciple's evangelized Jerusalem, Samaria and places throughout the known world.

I imagine Satan was having a hissy fit about the resurrection of the Christ. He had done all he could to derail the plan of God. He tried to kill Jesus as an infant, he tried to tempt Him to sin in the wilderness, he attempted to kill Him through the religious sects, and he tried to trick Him to say something that would cause his demise. He was just as unsuccessful with Jesus as He was with God. Because he wasn't successful with God the Father and God the Son, he turned up the heat to derail the men and women of the earth into a considerable life of sin filled with total disregard for human life and total disdain for the One Who sits on the throne.

Satan began having a field day with the nations of the world. He influenced men and women to reject God and serve, worship and fear a god made with their hands. Can you imagine that, forging a god to fear? He sent false prophets into the mist to encourage church members and everyone else that all gods were equal, legitimate and worthy of the praise from the people of the earth. Satan has always influenced men and women to hate others that don't look like them, talk like them or lived like them. The father of racism has been working for ages authoring strife between different nations, tribes, and cultures. For instance, African tribal wars were a constant. The winners, victors, or conqueror of these wars and battles gathered the defeated tribe and sold them to white slave traders who then sold them to plantation owners. Most of these plantation owners called themselves Christians but there wasn't any characteristics of the doctrine of Jesus portrayed in their lives. Even though they prayed to what they thought was a white god, they had no idea that if you don't love others then you don't even know God.

Today, there is a fair amount of children of slave owners who are still angry by the harsh treatment their relatives received by their slave masters. A lot of blacks will not come to Christianity and serve Jesus because the slave masters claimed to be Christian while raping wives, whipping their children, selling their property and just being mistreated as a whole. Years later, many Blacks have formed groups and organizations and even religions, made up of Satan inspired rules to protest against non-blacks. These particular Afro-

Introduction

Americans are living with strongholds that can only be destroyed by the One they don't trust. All cultures must let bad experiences go because it often affects our thought life and builds walls between each other. If we are focusing on what someone did to us in the past, then we are missing out of God's grace today, we are missing out of God's goodness today, we are missing out of God's love today, we are missing out on God's plan for our lives today.

On the flipside, there are many whites who believe black people are still 3/5 of a human being. These particular people believe they are superior to all other races. This is a lie. Some blacks are being discriminated on every level by white corporate America who believes in the lie. And there are still groups of racists killing people of every color, while claiming to belong to Christ. This too, is *a stronghold* created and operated by Satan.

If a race of people hates another race of people for what they've done in the past, then this race of people is living on the power of hatred instead of the power of Christ. God commands us to love and not hate for there will not be one hater of any race at the feet of Jesus in eternity.

These are just examples of the influence of Satan.

These strongholds are unbreakable thoughts in the minds of people who are void of the Holy Spirit, in blacks and whites and every other race, creed or color of people. These citizens of Earth have rejected Jesus and the love for THE TRUTH, when they do this, God gives them a *strong delusion* to believe whatsoever (lie) they want to believe.

These strong delusions are not limited to racism, but also homosexuality, religion, and those who are caught up in a sinful life. It starts with not believing in Christ as the Son of God, and then actions are taken to support these beliefs. Before you know it, you'll have a full blown devil dwelling inside you causing you to do whatsoever. Mind you, God sent these strong delusions on those who have no love for the truth and these delusions cannot be broken by any human means, but can only be dealt with through repentance and renewing one's mind with THE TRUTH of God's Word.

Note: All white people and black people are not demons and devil filled with racism and sin. I'm not trying to put a sin blanket on whites, blacks or any other nation of people. However, everyone will be judged by God on their personal acts, and not judged as a group of people or a nation. Believe it or not, there's an angel in Heaven writing down each and every one of our deeds whether good or bad. Some folks will have their bad deeds blotted out because they believe and gave their life to Jesus as the Son of God. Others who don't believe will have to bite the bullet and spend eternity separated from the God they hated, and Jesus whom they disbelieved, in a place of torment from then on!

The United States of America; the land of the free and home of the brave was declared to be a Christian nation years ago. The United States of America has been the *melting pot* for many years for people around the world to migrate. People from other countries escaped to the U.S. in order to live free and non-troubled lives; however the problem with these people from other countries is they brought their gods with them when they came. Japan brought the god Shinto and others with them, Chinese brought their god Guanyin and others with them, Africans brought their god Ashanti, Jade and other gods with them, South American people brought Aharaigichi and other gods with them, the Russians brought Lada and other gods with them and India brought Hindu and other gods with them, the English brought the spirits of pride and greed with them and many other carnal Christian beliefs. There are too many countries and gods to list that were carried to the land of the free and the home of the brave. These gods took up residence in the U.S.A. and began to evangelize U.S. citizens instead of the citizens evangelizing the new comers. The United States is no longer a Christian nation, but nation of false prophets and false teachers teaching its citizens it's okay to sin, it's okay to serve another god, and it's okay to practice abominations on every level and call ourselves blessed.

It's been a little over two thousand years since the Church was founded by the Apostles under the direction of the Holy Spirit. The Church grew daily in leaps and bounds with only a few hiccups with the Synagogue of the Freedmen, (Cyrenians and Alexandrians, and those from Cilicia and Asia), who incited the killing of Stephen. Then one of the first acts of deception within the believers was with Ananias and his wife Sapphira who attempted to deceive the Holy Spirit and Peter on a donation to the Church. Of course these two fell dead in their tracks.

The Church has had ups and downs since then. The one Church has splintered into many denominations in which most honor certain Scriptures to build a doctrine. Since then the Church has gone through a series of wars, the church also charged living believers money to pay for their dead loved ones entrance into Heaven, the church allowed false prophets and teachers access to congregations and so on. Then there's the home grown false prophets, false Christ, false teachers, false idols and cult leaders like Charles Manson, David Koresh, Shoko Asahara, Marshall Applegate, Jim Jones, Heaven's Gate, Alamo Christian, The Nuwaubian Nation, Yahweh Ben Yahweh, and too many others to mention. These false religions and cults focus on child sex slavery, and self-appointed gods. The theme to most false religions and cults is sex, money and power. This is a long way from loving God and your brothers unconditionally. It is a long way from praying for those in trouble, and healing the sick, raising the dead, visiting prisoners, and honoring Christ in our lives. Jesus said there will be *a falling away* and its happening before our eyes.

Today, the One Church has split into seven conditions: The Loveless Church, The Persecuted Church, The Compromising Church, the Corrupt Church, The Dead Church, the Faithful Church and the Lukewarm Church. These seven conditions of these churches are the characteristics of every church around the globe. All the churches are not the same, some are compromising churches while others are dead churches; some are faithful churches while others are lukewarm. These are real churches that existed in John's day and the same spirits of these churches in the first century are alive and well in today's Church.

Introduction

The purpose John wrote this epistle was to give assurance of *eternal life* to those who believe in Jesus as the Christ. He wanted to confirm our relationship with God, Jesus, The Holy Spirit, and with one another. There were times when people were not sure about Jesus, but John gave readers then and now the test of actually knowing Him. He also exposed the world for what it is and warned us from loving the things in the world and the deceptions in these last days. John urges us to allow the Holy Spirit to abide in us because the Holy Spirit is Truth and when we allow this, we are actually walking in victory.

John talked about knowing the *spirit of error* and knowing THE TRUTH which is vital for today's Christian. The only way to know the Spirit of error is to have our belief system grounded in the Truth. We do that by studying the Word of God but most importantly, living the Word of God by loving Him and loving our neighbors, brothers and sisters in Christ. It doesn't matter what your brother or sister's nationality, race, creed or color may be, true Christians love unconditionally while fake Christians love when it is to their advantage, or have something else but Jesus to gain. I can guarantee you there are fake Christians in every church around the world. It is not our job to seek out fake Christians because they will expose themselves, but we are to correct them when they speak contrary to God's Word. If they receive correction then we have gained a brother or sister, if not they will probably leave. The strength of His True and unadulterated Word will run off any and all that are faking and shaking in His Church.

We as the Body of Christ must wake up. We must prepare all believers with the doctrine of Christ. We must walk as He walked, teach as He taught, preach as He preached and live as He lived. We've got to shake off all things in our lives that aren't His and make it our goal to live a life without sin. There will not be any practicing sinners over in Glory. So if you are confessing yourself as a sinner today instead of a son or daughter of God, then you're in trouble and will find out the hard way that Jesus wasn't lying, the Holy Spirit wasn't telling us tall tales. So we must agree with what the Bible says, not the Quran, or the Mormon bible, or some jacked-legged preacher, cult leader, or any other representative of the world, but the sanctified Holy Scriptures given to us by God for holy living.

Today, we must not engage ourselves in Black and White issues, for when we do; we become preoccupied with the world and will miss out on God's goodness, God's instructions and God's grace. We cannot take part in the world's issues such as gay rights and marriages, gun control, global warming, or politics;

these people have chosen their lives for themselves, they may think they have Jesus but their lifestyle suggests otherwise; for in reality, they rejected Jesus and are now living on the devil's rabbit trails. We should not preoccupy, obsess, fixate, and waist our time on issues that will not do us any heavenly good. We need to reach the lost, feed the poor, visit prisoners, teach THE TRUTH and reject all lies and deceptive teachers and preachers who bring them. Remember, for those who don't have love for the truth, God will and has sent them a strong delusion to believe whatever they want to believe. Since we are in this world and not of this world, let's go about our Father's business and love our enemies, do good to those who curse you and hate you because you will be identified with Jesus. This life on Earth has limits, but eternity is forever. Don't let ungodly choices set reservations for you in a living hell.

Michael R. Hicks

God's Blueprint

A Complete Study in First John

Chapter 1

JESUS

That which was from the beginning,
– First John 1:1 NKJV

Before time began as we know it, there was absolutely nothing to see, nothing to hear, nothing to smell, nothing to touch and nothing to taste because there was nothing, but God the Father, God the Son and God the Holy Spirit. There wasn't a planet Earth, nor a solar system, and no universe. There was only darkness, blackness; a dark void of nothingness. If you've ever been in the middle of the ocean, or a desert in the middle of night, you can look across the sky and just see total darkness with the exception of the stars. Before time began, there were no stars because there was no sky—there was nothing but blackness. I call it *eternity past*, but God changed all that in six days.

Jesus was here before there was a here, He made here. He was before the beginning of time. He was in eternity past with the Father when time and seasons were created. As the earth was formed, Jesus

God's Blueprint

called seconds, minutes, hours, weeks, months, years, decades, centuries and millenniums in order for the earth to keep time. There is no time in eternity, only in the creation. In fact, the only [what we call] "time" in eternity, is swallowed up in forever.

> In the beginning was the Word, and the Word was with God, and the Word was God. He was in beginning with God. All things were made through Him, and without Him nothing was made that was made. – John 1:1-3

Jesus is the Word and He was with God in the beginning. Many people do not know Jesus as the One Who created all we see, smell, hear, taste and touch. From single cell organisms to multi-million celled creatures in the oceans, on land, under the ground, and in the air, Jesus called all things into existence. There is an immeasurable creative power in the Voice of the Trinity. The world was created by the power of the tongue. When Jesus called, (vocally), for the oceans, the mountains, the trees and all plant life to existence, they came to be. There were no machines, cranes, or scaffolds to form the earth, but He spoke it and the world was. It is interesting to note, whatever Jesus says comes to pass.

We see this exercise revealed in Genesis Chapter

22

Jesus

One when God said, *"Let there be light"* and light came into existence. *"Let there be a firmament, and divide the waters which were under the firmament from the waters which were above the firmament."* He spoke it and it came to be. He did the same with the grass, herbs, and fruits when He created the seed and entire growth process, also known as the "sowing and reaping" process. He called the sun and the moon, sea creatures, birds, cattle, beast of the field and all creeping things into existence. When Jesus says *"Let there be!"* it is going to be.

> He is the image of the invisible God, the first-born over all creation. – Colossians 1:15

When people read this passage of Scripture, some think carnally (in the natural) such as two people coming together to have a baby. However, Jesus was not born by fornication in the Spirit realm nor the earthly realm. God caused Jesus to exist before time was created. In John 8:42, Jesus says, *"I proceeded forth and came from God..."* To *proceed* is to 'come from or arise from something.' So Jesus came forth, or proceeded from God in eternity past. Now to be born is to come from a female but that is not the case here. Jesus was born of God somewhere in eternity past.

All things were made through Him, and without Him nothing was made that was made.

– John 1:3

Again, everything we see was created by God the Son by the spoken Word. Colossians 1:16 -18 reads:

> For by Jesus all things were created that are in heaven and that are on earth, visible and invisible, whether thrones or dominions or principalities or powers. All things were created through Jesus and for Jesus. And Jesus is before all things, and in Him all things consist. And Jesus is the head of the body, the church, who is the beginning, the firstborn from the dead, that in all things He may have the preeminence.

■ ■ ■

There is an immeasurable creative power in the Voice of the Trinity. The world was created by the power of the tongue.

Jesus created the spiritual power grid. The governments on Earth mirror the governments in the spiritual world. *Dominions* are governments; rulers (ruling powers), or authorities that are in control. It is also someone's area (sphere) of influence or control, e.g., a land governed by a ruler. *Principalities* are territories ruled by a prince or a princess.

Jesus

Preeminence is standing out among all others because of superiority. Jesus stands above and beyond everything everywhere; because, Jesus created everything everywhere. Through Jesus, all governments were established on Earth and in the spiritual realms. Again, there are governments in the heavens as there are governments on Earth—Jesus is Lord over them all.

The world was corrupted through the sin of Adam. That act of disobedience in the garden has caused the earth to be as it is today, corrupt, dishonest, fraudulent, and crooked. There are good people and bad people mixed around the globe; however, even the good people were born in sin. Since the world was [and is] full of sin, and everyone is born with a sin nature, we need a Savior to get us back to God's intent for mankind. The actions of men didn't surprise God, nor did it catch Him off guard, nor creep upon Him. He knew man would fail and live their lives full of wrath, devastations, and pure unadulterated sin. So God sent Jesus into the earth to offer mankind salvation from their sins. Whoever believes in Jesus as the Son of God will receive a lifetime of fellowship with God the Father, God the Son and God the Holy Spirit in this life and in the next life!

He was in the world, and the world was made

through Him, and the world did not know Him. He came to His own, and His own did not receive Him. But as many as received Him, to them He gave the right to become children of God, to those who believe in His name: who were born, not of blood or the will of the flesh, nor of the will of man but of God. – John 1:10-13

Even though Jesus made the earth and all that is in it, when He came into the world, the world did not know Him. He came to help the world escape from their sins, but the world did not receive Him. In fact, they came against Him, because He told mankind we are sinners and need to change our lives. He was resented, hated and was shown antipathy for His kindness and for calling it as it was; to the end He was eventually crucified for it. But for those who believe in Him, He gave us a *legal right* (emphasis mine) to become sons of God. This is not done by the will or plans of man, it's not done through fornication, but by the will of God, the born again experience. We were born in sin, but born again by the Spirit of God only!

A lot of people wonder why God allows sin to run wild in governments, countries, and cities and the people in them to live corrupt lives. Some believe God does not exist because of all the violence and sin that abounds in the land. But Jesus doesn't rule over these governments as men understand ruling; such as presidents, prime ministers, kings or princes. The plan of the Trinity is that every male and female born of a woman would have the chance to *choose* to serve *either* God or the enemy of the Trinity; it's just that simple. For those who choose God through Jesus Christ, they will be blessed and will receive eternal life. While those who do not choose God and reject Jesus will also live forever; but it won't be in Heaven. Contrastly, their life will continue in a Lake of Fire— from now on. So the consequences of those who reject Jesus are the complete opposite of those who accept Jesus. One is cursed while the other is blessed.

Jesus is the head of the true Church, He doesn't have anything to do with churches that are not obedient to His Word, nor love their brother; except, to judge them for their actions on Judgment Day. He is the power of the Church, the wisdom of the Church and the love of the Church. Jesus should be the Lord of all our lives. Every Christian leader should acknowledge Jesus as Lord, teach Jesus as Lord, and live accordingly, because Jesus is Lord. We should not seek our own wisdom, but the wisdom of Christ. We should seek Jesus as a drowning man seeks air, for we cannot live successfully without Him.

God's Blueprint

Chapter 2

THE BEGINNING OF MINISTRY

T hat which was from the beginning, which we have heard, which we have seen with our eyes, which we have looked upon, and our hands have handled, concerning the Word of Life – the life was manifested, and we have seen, and bear witness, and declare to you that eternal life which was with the Father and was manifested to us – that which we have seen and heard we declare to you, that you also may have fellowship with us; and truly our fellowship is with the Father and with His Son Jesus Christ. And these things we write to you that your joy may be complete. – First John 1:1-4 NKJV

For years, mankind has heard of God basically through the Nation of Israel. God showed Himself mightily throughout their generations as a provider, a healer, and a deliverer and in many other ways. When the fullness of time came, God the Father sent God the Son to the earth as Emmanuel, to manifest the fact that God is real. To *manifest* is to make known what was previously not known. The twelve disciples knew of God, but had no idea of the Son of God until He came and made Himself known as the Son of God. What was invisible was now visible, what was not known is now known. The disciple's testimony is they had been with the Son of God. They looked upon Him and they touched Him and declared eternal life is here and now our fellowship is available with God the Father and God the Son.

Jesus revealed Himself to twelve men; eleven of them turned the world upside down. The testimonies of the eleven disciples were not hearsay but they were actual witnesses to the Word of Life. For three years, they followed Him and watched in awe the miracles He performed. They watched Him walk on water and pay taxes from the mouth of a fish. They watched Him heal the sick by the multitudes, they witnessed Him raise the dead at least twice, they watched in wonder as He healed lepers and calmed a raging sea. These are events they would never forget, and they gave witness of the works and the Words of Christ to whosoever was present at the time or would later listen. It is possible a few of the disciples, (before they were actually disciples) were there at the baptism of Jesus when the Voice came from Heaven, ***"This is My beloved Son in***

Whom I'm well pleased." (See: Mt 3:17) And in Luke 9:35, Peter, James, and John heard God's approval of Jesus and instructions on the Mount of Transfiguration, *"This is My beloved Son, hear Him!"*

■ ■ ■

We should seek Jesus as a drowning man seeks air, for we cannot live successfully without Him.

The purpose of *witnessing,* is to share Christ with people who don't know Him and fellowship with those who believe. But the greatest blessing of it all is we get to fellowship with God the Father and God the Son. When believers fellowship with one another we also are fellowshipping with God and Jesus, so that our joy may be complete in Him. So, in this passage John testifies and encourages believers to enjoy fellowship with God, Jesus and all other believers.

The Eternal Life which was manifested in the person of Jesus the Christ—has changed the world.

God's Blueprint

Chapter 3

A FALSE CLAIM

There were some false claims that were spreading throughout Judea attacking Jesus and the Gospel. These false prophets were spreading damaged and and flawed teachings in the first century, just as they are today. The first one is: claiming to walk in the light or have fellowship with God; while, failing to live in His moral, ethical, honorable, and honest character.

> This is the message which we have heard from Him and declare to you, that God is light and in Him is no darkness at all. – First John 1:5 NKJV

John's message is 'God is Light'. According to Strong's Bible Concordance, *'Light'* is, "to shine or make manifest." God is pure light, the Author and epitome of light. *God's light* refers to His moral character and there is no darkness in God at all! God is holy, unapproachable, and untouched by evil or sin. There is no confusion, no blindness, no deceit, no ulterior motive, no error, no ignorance, no stupidity, and certainly no racism in God. There is no darkness in God at all, nor can there be, because God is the quintessence, embodiment, and personification of light and that light is unadulterated but, it always exposes and conquers the darkness.

> If we say that we have fellowship with Him, and walk in darkness, we lie and do not practice the truth. But if we walk in the light as He is in the light, we have fellowship with one another and the blood of Jesus Christ His Son cleanses us from all sin. – 1 John 1:6-7

To walk in darkness is to live contrary to God's moral character. If we make the claim, "We have fellowship with God," without living a moral or honorable life by practicing the truth, is to live—A LIE. If we say we are a Christian and walking in the light, or that we have fellowship with God, but yet we're gossiping, lying, having sex outside of marriage, committing adultery, stealing, murdering, participating in same sex relationships (as a man with a woman), practicing racism and hatred, serving other gods, practicing witchcraft, disobedient to God's commands; or agree with anyone who practices these vices, we are not practicing the truth, but walking in darkness. Basically put, he who practices sin, is a sinner and he who does not practice sin is a child of God.

A False Claim

A pure example is when an actor or a singer receives an award on television for some extraordinary performance. The first thing most winners say is, "I'd like to thank God!" However, the material, the song, or the movie part they won the award for is totally opposite of God's moral character. Like a sinner thanking God for the award in which foul language was displayed with sinister actions, unclean philosophies, anti-Christ ideals, and untruths about the Word of God. They may thank God for the talent, but they disrespect Him by their actions, even if it was fiction.

■ ■ ■

If we make the claim, "We have fellowship with God," without living a moral or honorable life by practicing the truth, is to live—A LIE.

To have fellowship with God is like having a relationship with your spouse, family member, or a very close friend; only better. A relationship is built on love, trust, loyalty, openness, dependability, devotion, and faithfulness. To have fellowship with God is to spend time with God. The more time we spend with God, the stronger our relationship will become.

To walk in the light is to live in a manner of truth with

God's Blueprint

God. When a believer reflects God's moral character, then there will be real fellowship with other Christians. Our fellowship with God depends on living, or walking in God's light, or living in His moral character. It is here that sin is revealed in our lives, but the good news is the revelation brings us to Christ. Only the blood of the Christ can cleanse us from all our sins. The Bible doesn't say Jesus covered our sins or just touched us up; He completely cleansed us from our sins. In short Jesus cleanses us and made us spotless, unsoiled, and sin free. When Jesus cleanses a person from sin, then he/she is no longer in sin—it's been washed away. The person does not have any sin any longer because Jesus cleansed, took away, and thoroughly obliterated our sin nature. Now, there may have been times when a cleansed person decides to go back into their old life. And when they do, they are eight times worse than they were before they were cleansed of their sins.

> If we say we have no sin, we deceive ourselves, and the truth is not in us. If we confess our sins, He is faithful and just to forgive us sin and to cleanse us from all unrighteousness. If we say we have not sinned, we make Him a liar, and His word is not with us. – 1 John 1:8-10

Another false claim of the day is, "we have no sin." If

A False Claim

we say we have no sin, or we have never sinned then we are liars and there's no truth dwelling in us. We were all liars before we came to Jesus and when we confess our sins, Jesus is faithful to first, forgive your sin and, second cleanse you from all *unrighteousness,* which is lack of virtue, lack of godly morality and lack of honesty. When this is done, we are the righteousness of God in Christ Jesus. When Jesus causes us to be His righteousness in God we are of good quality, good value, good worth, and of high merit.

If we say we have not sinned, then we are actually calling God a liar. But God is ALL TRUTH and there's not an iota of lying in Him. If we say we have not sinned, we will not be a child of God and His Word will not be with us. Also if we say we haven't sinned, then we've lost out on Heaven and have gained a one way ticket to Hell and the Lake of Fire. Again, when we live in God's moral character, we will have fellowship with God and His children. When we have fellowship with God, the blood of Jesus Christ cleanses us from all sin.

If we say we have no sin, we deceive ourselves
and the truth is not in us. − 1 John 1:8

If we have no sin then there would be no need for Jesus to get off His throne and come down from Heaven to

God's Blueprint

die for our sins. We were born with a sin nature, we did not have to go to the School of Sin to learn the ins and outs of practicing unrighteousness, and we didn't have any Sin 101 classes to show us the way. Our sin nature urged us to lie naturally, to steal naturally, to practice the lust of the flesh naturally, the lust of the eyes naturally, and the pride of life naturally, and the lust to practice all unrighteousness naturally. If we believe we have never sinned then we are deceiving ourselves, misleading ourselves and we have no truth in us, because we do not have Jesus in us.

■ ■ ■

The person does not have any sin any longer because Jesus cleansed, took away, and thoroughly obliterated our sin nature.

Self-deception is a terrible way to live and when a person persist in living a life of deception, then God will give this person a *strong delusion* to believe whatever they want to believe.

> And for this reason God will send them a strong delusion that they should believe the lie.
> – Thessalonians 2:11

If a man persists to believe he's a girl then God will

A False Claim

allow him to think just that. God's not okay with it, but He won't interfere because the person has a choice to believe the truth or to believe a lie. When His Word is rejected, these people will wholehearted embrace a lie as the truth. A man or woman will undergo procedures to strengthen his illusion of who he thinks he is, he will change his mannerisms, his speech pattern and his entire way of life and will freely live the delusion he believed in his flesh.

> For by grace you have been saved through faith, and that not of yourselves; it is the gift from God, not of works, lest anyone should boast.
> – Ephesians 2:8-9

God's divine influence upon our hearts has saved us through our faith in Christ Jesus. This is something we could not do on our own, we couldn't save ourselves, we needed a divine power to change our evil nature to a holy nature. Some believe that whipping ourselves with a bullwhip can cleanse us from unrighteousness or abstaining from food or even refraining from sex can save us; while still, others think their works can save them, but that is not true. Some believe if they give enough money, they can make into the pearly gates. Others believe if they just go to church once a week they'll be Heaven bound. We cannot save ourselves through good works: such as

God's Blueprint

feeding the poor or giving finances to the down and out. We cannot buy or give our way into Heaven. We cannot be saved by going to church every week and sitting on the third row and shout a ritualistic amen on queue. We cannot save ourselves by facing the east to pray, or by developing rituals that can bring us to salvation. Marching around the black rock in Mecca seven times will not save you but condemn you. Bowing down to worship images of wood, stone, cars, houses, money or anything that was created cannot bring us to salvation. Only the grace of God, (God's divine influence in our hearts), can save us. We are saved by our faith in Jesus Christ.

Chapter 4
THE SIN DILEMMA

F or all have sinned and fall short of the glory of God. – Romans 3:23 NKJV

Every human being on the planet has sinned several times in the duration of our lives. Every last one of us has lied, stole something, or coveted someone's property, wife or husband. We've gossiped about someone, while still others have murdered, hated, raped, or molested someone. It doesn't matter if you told a lie, (white lie or black lie), because all lies will keep you from obtaining eternal life, or if you killed thousands of people; the reality is, sin is sin and to God there is no big sin or little sin. There is no difference between a gossip and a killer. Each and every one of us have sinned and brought disapproval, condemnation and even the wrath of God on our lives.

And she will bring forth a Son, and you shall call His name Jesus, for He will save His people from their sins. – Matthew 1:21

God's Blueprint

The virgin Mary gave birth to Jesus and God told her to name Him—Jesus. The main purpose Jesus came to the earth was to save us from our sin, to reconcile us with the Father and create an opportunity for every living soul to have eternal life. Not only did He come to save us from our sins, and take the wrath of God off our lives; but also, to teach us to love one another. In addition, He taught us how to live righteous lives, and how to worship the Father and pray to God the Father. Since Jesus came to save us from our sins, why do we think we can still live a life of sin? I've heard a lot of people declare they're saved, but they still sin. To me, this is an oxymoron and it's statements like these that make you want to pull your hair out. I wonder how God feels about sending his Son to die for our sins, cleanse us from all unrighteousness and yet we continue proclaiming we are still sinners. Now there are times when we make a mistake, slip up or mess up, but that's not what we're talking about—that's not practicing sin.

> But God demonstrates His love toward us, in that while we were still sinners, Christ died for us,
> – Romans 5:8

God did not wait for the people of the earth to achieve a godly character, He couldn't wait, because we were all evil, and it was impossible for us to live a holy life without the Holy One. So God the Father sent God the Son to Earth, while we were all living evil, sinful lives and He demonstrated, established and verified His love toward us in order for us to receive His salvation and to live a Holy and righteous life.

■ ■ ■

God's divine influence upon our hearts has saved us through our faith in Christ Jesus. This is something we could not do on our own, we couldn't save ourselves, we needed a divine power to change our evil nature to a holy nature.

This is actually the ultimate faith because we were no good at all; but Christ looked beyond our messy lives, beyond our faults and became a man to die as a sacrifice for our sins. Jesus has never, ever committed an evil act of unrighteousness or sin. Satan tried to tempt Jesus into sin in Matthew 4, Mark 1:12, and Luke 4, but he was unsuccessful. The devil thought, because Jesus was made flesh and dwelt among men, he could catch Him off guard after spending forty days and forty nights in the dessert without food or water and trick Him into sin. The devil had been successful influencing many men to sin during the ages; however, he came up short on his schemes against Christ. In

God's Blueprint

the Book of Hebrews the writer informs us…

> For in that He Himself has suffered, being tempted, He is able to aid those who are tempted.
> — Romans 2:18

When Jesus was a man, He ate like men, drank like men, use the restroom like men, slept like men, and He walked like men. He was tempted in every area of life but did not sin. I'm sure the devil may have sent a woman or two to cause Him to sin but He never indulged and never sinned. So Jesus knows what we're going through, and He knows *the wiles of the devil* and the plight of men. He came to be the perfect answer for us because He has gone through everything we are going through in life—He just didn't sin.

> What shall we say then? Shall we continue in sin that grace may abound? Certainly not! How shall we who died to sin live any longer in it? Or do you not know that as many of us as were baptized into Christ Jesus were baptized into death? Therefore we were buried with Him through baptism into death that just as Christ was raised from the dead by the glory of the Father, even so we should walk in newness of life.
> — Romans 6:1-4

The Sin Dilemma

For some folks, sin seems to be the way for God's grace to be enacted in our lives, (the more we sin the more grace we get from God), and so why not continue to sin that grace, (God's divine influence on the hearts of men) can increase, proliferate, and enlarge in our lives. The grace of God does not give us carte blanche to sin. Actually it is just the opposite, when we gave our lives to Christ (or were born again), we became dead to sin. The baptism of Jesus the Messiah, Jesus the Christ is *a blueprint* for everyone who would come to Him. Jesus did not have to be baptized, but He did for righteousness sake. His water baptism is a sign for the new believer of burial when He went in the water and resurrection when He came up from the water. It is an example of His burial in His tomb and His resurrection from the grave on the third day. We as a Christian Nation also died when He went into the grave and we also were resurrected when He arose from the grave. This process is the foundation for all Believers to be dead from sins and to walk in the newness of life.

> For if we have been united together in the likeness of His death, certainly we also shall be in the likeness of His resurrection, knowing this that our old man was crucified with Him, that the body of sin might be done away with, that we should no longer be slaves to sin. – Romans 6:5-6

God's Blueprint

From the time we were born to the time we came to Christ for salvation, we were dead people walking. We didn't have God, Jesus or the Holy Spirit. We were spinning our lives away in sin as we were working on our wages of sin. When Christ saved us—our lives changed and we aren't the same person we used to be. I can attest to this, I was a spiritual imbecile while I worked on my wages of sin exclusively, until I gave my life to Christ. Now I am a completely different person and the Kingdom of God is my agenda.

■ ■ ■

He came to be the perfect answer for us because He has gone through everything we are going through in life — He just didn't sin.

When we go through this process, our old man dies (our sinful nature) so that our bodies of sin could be done away with. When we unite with Christ, we're no longer slaves to sin because there's no sin in Christ. When we were slaves to sin, we didn't have a choice but to sin. The devil directed our lives as a puppeteer to sin as he wished. So when Jesus died, we died with Him, when He arose, we arose with Him so we are no longer slaves to sin. We are no longer a puppet for the devil.

The Sin Dilemma

For the death that He died, He died to sin once and for all; but the life that He lives, He lives to God. Likewise, you also reckon yourselves to be dead indeed to sin, but alive to God in Christ Jesus our Lord. Verses 10-11

Jesus is not going to get on the cross and die for our sins again. Jesus died for all people who lived before the crucifixion, during the season of His crucifixion, and for thousands of years after His crucifixion. The life Jesus lived is a life for God and, it is God's desire for the people of the earth to be born again and to live a life dead to sin. Because of what He did, born again believers need to reckon themselves, consider themselves, imagine themselves living a life of believing we are dead to sin and alive to Christ. This is not Michaelology—this is God's Word, the Bible.

Let's imagine we're standing in front of a coffin with a dead person in it. We can try to feed the dead person but he/she won't respond. We can attempt communication, but there's no response. We can play their favorite song, but there will be no response. We can even shoot, stab, or burn the dead person but there will not be any response because the person is dead and dead people cannot respond to anything. As the departed is dead to life, we should be dead to sins.

God's Blueprint

In Him we have redemption through His blood, the forgiveness of sins, according to the riches of His grace. – Ephesians 1: 7

Now that we are in Christ Jesus, we have redemption, deliverance, and liberation. We have been bought, purchased, acquired, paid for, and obtained by the blood of Christ and we now belong to Him. He is our Lord, our Master, and our big Brother. There cannot be any redemption without the shedding of blood and Jesus shed His blood in order for us to be forgiven of all our sins. We are no longer under the wrath of God but protected as sons and daughters of the King. We also received the richness of God's divine influence upon our hearts, when God gives, He gives liberally.

For if we sin willingly after we have received the knowledge of the truth, there no longer remains a sacrifice for sins. – Hebrews 10:26

If a person gives his life to Christ, is baptized and born again, has been taught the ways of the covenant and received the knowledge of the truth, and then goes back to a life of sin, he has done the worst possible thing in the world. To return to a sin filled life will be spiritual suicide. There no longer remains a sacrifice for sins for this person. For this person, Jesus died for nothing, He was beaten for nothing, He was whipped for nothing, and He gave up His Spirit at the cross for nothing. This person would be an idiot and a fool to reject Jesus after coming to the knowledge of the truth.

Satan will attempt to plant pop-ups in your mind of bad deeds in your history. We have to put these pop- ups to rest immediately, and we must refuse to dwell on our old evil life. If you dwell on these thoughts, (replay your past sins in your mind), you will be back in the game of death before too long. Remember, they are not your thoughts; they are the thoughts of Satan's influence trying to lure and seduce you back into his kingdom. He's trying to sway your mind into thinking you've done bad things that could never be forgiven. If you do take heed to these extreme and evil thoughts, you will find yourself eight times worse than you were before you were delivered. (See: Mt 12:43)

> For it is impossible for those who were once enlighten, and have tasted the heavenly gift, and have become partakers of the Holy Spirit, and have tasted the good word of God and the powers to come, if they fall away, to renew them again to repentance, since they crucify again for themselves the Son of God, and put Him to open shame. – Hebrews 6:4-6

God's Blueprint

One of the most solemn warnings against *apostasy* found in the Scriptures is to willingly forsake Christ Jesus after coming into the knowledge of the truth. This person has literally disqualified his/her life and signed up with the devil because there is no repentance for the sins committed by this person. This person has rejected a life of love and peace for a life of calamity. There is no more repentance for this person. There is no more spiritual order for this person. There is no more pure love for this person. There is only Hell and the Lake of Fire for this person in the next life.

■ ■ ■

Jesus is not going to get on the cross and die for our sins again.

It's sad to say there are millions who live for this, they love living in blindness but they believe they can see. They love debating and arguing because it's a way of life without any purpose, closure or end. If a person falls away from the life of Christ and goes back to a life of sin after he has learned the truth, there will not be a comeback for this person. Some believe in the Burger King philosophy, you can live life your own way, or you can have it your way. I'm here to tell you that you can live your life your own way but the wages of your lifestyle will condemn you to the Lake of Fire. There will be a price to pay for our actions, whether good or bad.

50

The Sin Dilemma

Jesus willingly, eagerly, and freely gave His life for mankind to save us from our sins and made it possible for us to live a life without practicing sin. Why would anyone want to go back to a dreaded lifestyle of sin and darkness where blindness, confusion, rebellion, spiritual error and ignorance are the chief character traits?

> Jesus answered them, "Most assuredly, I say to you, whoever commits sin is a slave to sin.
> – John 8:34

Slaves have no rights. When a person commits sin, then the devil is his/her master. *Masters* can do whatever they want to their slaves, they can work them from sun up to sun down; they can treat them harshly, treat them cruelly, beat them, rape them (both men and women), sell them, produce babies with them, torture them and even kill them. Slaves want to be free but they're unable to go free, because their master has a stronghold in their minds. Strongholds in the minds of people are flooded with acts of sin and rebellion against everything. The mind is guarded by Satan and will not allow the person to be free of his tutelage, his guidance or his auspices. When Satan manipulates a person's mind, then the person will be the devil's slave. Satan is the slave master of people who do not know Christ. He manipulates the carnal and the natural into sinning against humanity. People are living in foul and terrible circumstances and don't know why. People are angry and don't know why. People are killing one another, raping one another, beating, whipping and disfiguring one another and don't know why. People are killing themselves through drugs and alcohol and sexual diseases and don't know why. People are practicing hatred on one another and don't know why. People are sinning to the fullest and don't know why. People are sinning because they don't know Jesus and are slaves to sin; because they are under the influence of Satan. So when you see these actions displayed on the Six O'clock, you'll know Satan has influenced their minds because they are slaves to sin.

The only One Who could break down these strongholds, deliver people with slave mentalities of darkness, Who can break the chains of sin, and free us from being spiritual depraved is Jesus the Christ. Jesus can take whoever is a slave to sin and change him/her into a child of God.

Chapter 5
OUR ADVOCATE

My little children, these things I write to you, so that you may not sin. And if anyone sins, we have an Advocate with the Father, Jesus Christ the righteous. And He Himself is the propitiation for our sins, and not for our sins only but also for the whole world.
                                        – First John 2:1 NKJV

Information is absolutely essential for the brothers and sisters in Christ. John, the fatherly Apostle still teaches us today about spiritual matters. Sin never goes away and is ever present throughout this entire world. Even though we are born again Christians, sin still lurks around every corner looking for the opportunity to entice us back into the dark life of sin.

If we ever find ourselves caught up in a sinful situation, we have an Advocate, a supporter, a backer, or a campaigner who goes before God the Father on our behalf. Jesus, our advocate is our legal representative in the heavenly court room. An *advocate* is one called to our side. He supports us because we believe He is the Son of God, Who came to set us free from evil, sin and the grave. He came to take away our sins in order to present us to Father God as holy, blameless and without a blemish. The whole world has the opportunity to receive God's blessing, but unfortunately most of the world will reject Jesus and God and refuse to be free of the devil's interest.

■ ■ ■

Jesus can take whoever is a slave and change him/her into a child of God.

Propitiation brings about the merciful removal of guilt through divine forgiveness. *Propitiation* is to appease, or make peace with, or pacify somebody to someone. In this case, Jesus had to appease God for our sins. Since there is no appeasement without the shedding of blood – Jesus became our *propitiation*. In the Old Testament, the High Priest sprinkled blood with a hyssop branch on the mercy seat to appease God's holy wrath against the men and women of Israel. A little over two thousand years ago, God sent His Son, to satisfy His own wrath by sending Jesus to the earth to sacrifice His life on the cross. Our sins made it necessary for Jesus to suffer the agony, anguish, torture, suffering and distress of the crucifix-

Our Advocate

ion.   So God demonstrated His love and justice by
providing His own Son. That sacrifice of Jesus' sinless
life was so effective that it supplies forgiveness for the
entire world. The death of Christ is sufficient for everyone who believes in Him. It is available to all, even
though many will not accept it.

God's Blueprint

Chapter 6

THE TEST OF KNOWING GOD

Now by this we know that we know Him, if we keep His commandments. He who says, "I know Him," and does not keep His commandments, is a liar, and the truth is not in him. – First John 2:3-4 NKJV

The confidence of knowing God is to keep His commandments. When God is our top priority, we are able to keep His commandments which are to love Him and love our neighbors as we love ourselves. We need to know that only those who are learning to live like Jesus, are the ones who know Him and love Him. When we truly love God then we'll truly know Him. Now God knew us before the beginning of time, before the foundation of the earth, and this is a great honor that God bestows upon His children. So when we love God, we'll know God and we will experience His goodness, His nature, His grace, His wisdom, His peace, and His protection on a personal level. When we keep these commandments, we're blessed. But if we say, "We know God but do not keep His commandments," then we are liars and there's not a shred of truth within us. It is a terrible thing to be a liar, to live an empty life filled with empty exasperations, frustrations, and anger. The evidence of people who don't know God is on The News every night expressing their mayhem, their hatred, their confusion, their havoc and pandemonium for their fellow man. You may think you have peace, but you've deceived yourself because your peace comes from the world, and the world's peace is not real, but is flaky, false, and insecure. The only real peace comes from God.

Obedience to the commandments of God's will test one's knowledge of Him. Genuine love for God and true knowledge of Him must be evident by your loyalty to Him. This loyalty comes from choosing God and His ways in every situation, in every test, and in every conflict. We must choose to walk and converse with others demonstrating God's moral character. Even if we are in a bad situation, we must choose to use the knowledge of God as our defense. This won't work if you don't read your Bible and haven't allowed the Holy Scriptures to live in your heart. This knowledge will not be a mental assent or hearsay but will manifest as your relationship with Him grows. You won't be guessing about the knowledge of God through fables, allegories and myths, because you know Him personally through your prayers, His Word, and the Holy Spirit that dwells in you.

It is impossible for a liar to tell the truth about anything. Falsehoods flow from a liar's mouth like water plunges from Victoria Falls. Liars have the ability to look you in the eye and fabricate *a version* of the truth on a moment's notice. In these Last Days' false pastors, false bishops, false teachers and false prophets will look you in the eye and tell you "God is dead, or Jesus is not the Son of God or Jesus did not come from Heaven in the flesh, or there are many roads to Heaven, or Christianity is a farce full of pie in the sky dreams." These people are liars and in league with the antichrist. As believers, we need to keep His commandments because His commandments are life and truth and our daily experiences with Him builds a relationship of truth that stands the test of time.

> But whoever keeps His word, truly the love of God is perfected in him. By this we know that we are in Him. He who says he abides in Him ought himself also to walk just as He walked.
> – 1 John 2:5-6

To *keep His Word* is to be active in maintaining your life in His Word every day. Not just on Sunday or

God's Blueprint

just one day a week or even two, but every day we should maintain, uphold, sustain, and continue our lives in His Word. It is to be obedient to the plans of God as Jesus was obedient to God's plan. We are perfected with each and every obedient act of righteousness, morality, honesty, and virtue; it is the very act of kindness and love for our fellow men and women. To be perfected is to be without fault, complete, whole, excellent, especially suitable, skilled, and absolute. When we know God and keep His Word, His love will be perfected in us. In the eyes of God, we'll be without fault; we'll be complete, whole, excellent, and especially suitable, because we love on God and He loves on us. By this we know we abide in Him and He abides in us. Believers are truly blessed because the Father dwells in our spirits. Without God we're nothing, but with God we're everything we need to be and what He wants us to be. When we realize this, we can truly walk as Jesus walked.

He who says he's in the light, and hates his brother, is in darkness until now. He who loves his brother abides in the light, and there is no cause for stumbling in him. But he who hates his brother is in darkness, and does not know where he is going, because the darkness has blinded his eyes. – 1 John 2:2-11

The Test of Knowing God

When a Christian declares he/she is living in the light, or living in God's moral character but they hate their brother or sister, they are living a lie. They are not abiding in the light because their hatred for their brother has moved them into the darkness. A person cannot live in the darkness and in the light at the same time. It's going to be one or the other; light or darkness.

■ ■ ■

Genuine love for God and true knowledge of Him must be evident by your loyalty to Him.

God requires us to love our sisters and brothers. He's given us the Holy Spirit so that we can love one another without any hidden agendas. This love, *agape* is a supernatural, unconditional love, godly love that we must practice and live by. When we live in agape, and abiding in the love of Christ, there's no cause to stumble, stagger, or falter in our walk with Christ.

A person who hates his brother is in opposition to Christ's teachings. Even the idea of claiming fellowship with God while hating one's brother shows thoughts and actions that are truly generated by the devil of darkness. Living in darkness is living in ignorance, blindness, disobedience and rebellion. When

God's Blueprint

a Christian has hatred in their hearts, they'll have no idea where they are going and won't be able to see the truth even if it is staring them in the eye. As we know, living in darkness is living in sin.

There are nations of people who say they love God but they hate Americans. It is probably true about their love for God but they have the wrong god. There are many gods around the world and they all promote hatred toward their brothers and sisters and everybody else. God is a God of love and not hate. The Aryan Brotherhood and the Klan claims to be Christians but they hate other races in Christ Jesus. They truly believe they are serving God, praying to God to keep a pure white race with a touch of superiority. On Judgment Day they will find out they were far from the truth of God's Word. It's extremely difficult to read the Word of God and still have hate in your heart.

Chapter 7

THE BLUEPRINT

J esus did not step out of eternity onto Earth just to save us from our sins. He did not come to Earth just to heal us and deliver us and show us great signs and wonders. He didn't come just to walk on the water He created, or pull coins for taxes from the mouth of a fish. He did not come to Earth just to give us life and life more abundantly. Indeed, Jesus accomplished all these things. All of these are important because it is the plan of God and His plan hasn't changed. The reason Jesus came was to give us the blueprint for life, ministry, and eternal life. He came to give us the recipe for Godly living. And He started teaching us God's blueprint by being an example for us.

Let this mind be in you which was also in Christ Jesus, who being in the form of God; did not consider it robbery to be equal with God, but made Himself of no reputation, taking the form of a bondservant, and coming in the likeness of men. And being found in appearance as a man, He humbled Himself and became obedient to the point of death, even death of the cross. – 2 Philippians 2:5-9

Let this mind be in you...

All godly actions begin with *the renewing of the mind.* We renew our mind by meditating and rolling the instructions of Christ over and over in our minds until it becomes alive in our spirits. The Word of God strengthens believers into thinking good or right thoughts. Right thinking produces right actions. Bad thinking or stinking thinking produces bad actions. The actions of believers are the fruits of our deepest thoughts. God is the author of our deepest thoughts and He lines us up with divine appointments in order for us to bear good fruit. The more we meditate on the Word of God, the more sensitive we become to His Voice, the stronger we become in Christ Jesus. We also become useful as Kingdom builders for Him. Thinking and being like Christ are requirements for believers. If we are not thinking and living as Christ, then we need to examine our relationship, repent and yield to Him so that we may be strengthened and get back on the right track. As the Body of Christ, we need to think and act like one being, because Jesus the Christ, God the Father and God the Holy Spirit are One.

The Blueprint

Let this mind be in you which was also in Christ Jesus, who being in the form of God, did not consider it robbery to be equal with God but made Him of no reputation, taking on the form of a bondservant. – Philippians 2:5

Because Christ was/is God the Son, He did not look on sharing God's nature as robbery, or something to be seized as if He didn't already possess the nature of God. He had been with God since eternity past and will be with Him for eternity future. Since Christ is God the Son, it did not bother Him or trouble Him to be sharing His Father's nature because God the Father, God the Son, and God the Holy Ghost are One. He was already God the Son, full of everything that God is. But Jesus didn't trip, ponder, contemplate, or think it over; He made Himself of no reputation, He just emptied Himself of His Godly power and came to Earth as a mere man. He laid down His privileges as God and took the form of a servant. The Son of God/Son of man, Jesus was still the Son of God in title, but He was as powerless as any man when He was born of Mary.

And the child grew and became strong in spirit, filled with wisdom; and the grace of God was upon Him. – Luke 2:40

God's Blueprint

Jesus, as the mere human boy had to grow in order to be strong in spirit, his human spirit, not the Spirit of God. He was learning and become wise and the grace of God was upon Him. Jesus knew Who He was but still had to go through all the preliminaries and the mechanics of a child, learning of God. We have more in common than we think with Jesus. Just as Jesus grew and became strong in Spirit, we have to grow in the Lord to be strong in Spirit; likewise, as Jesus grew and became wise, we have the ability to grow also and become wise. Jesus spent time with God and we must spend time with God. The grace that was on Jesus is the same grace that is on and indwells every believer. Whatever Jesus did, we must do to be Christ like.

■ ■ ■

The reason Jesus came was to give us the blueprint for life, ministry, and eternal life. He came to give us the recipe for Godly living.

One day when Jesus was 12 year old, he lingered behind his family's caravan and spent time at the temple in Jerusalem. Jesus had been sitting in the midst of the teachers, both listening and asking them questions. The Bible says those who heard Him were astonished at His understanding and His an-

The Blueprint

swers. They were amazed, surprised, and probably even flabbergasted by His knowledge of the Scriptures. We know the teachers had to wonder where this twelve-year-old kid came from and wondered how He became acquainted with Spiritual matters of such great magnitude. Just as the Sanhedrin came to understand that Peter and John had been with Jesus, these teachers should have realized this twelve year old boy had been with God.

For the first thirty years as a mere man Jesus was absent of the power of God, Jesus humbled Himself and took the role of a servant in order to experience what man feels through the annals of human lives. His flesh had to feel the ups and downs, the joy and the disappointments men and women face every day. He witnessed the anguish of men; the suffering of men with all the pain, grief, torment, and sorrow. That's why He came in the flesh, because He couldn't have felt these raw emotions, temptations, and the lure of sin as God; because—God can't be tempted. He *identified* with the struggles of man on all levels of human life. I imagine sin was always at the door in attempts to redirect Him off the course God planned for Him: He had to experience them as a man. In fact, He wanted to identify with the struggles of man in all areas of life. In this way, He would become the proper advocate for believers today.

God's Blueprint

All the flesh centered religious groups tested Him in an attempt to cause Him to fail, or to blaspheme, or swear against God's Holy Word. They tried every way possible in attempts to cause Him to fall and stumble. But He never did. There may have been an endeavor to send a prostitute to Him in an attempt to get His mind off of His mission and into darkness. Sex is one of the devil's most potent and successful weapons through the years, it worked on Israel almost at will, and the nations on the earth was eating out of Satan's hand, but Jesus never sinned at any point.

Jesus went to John the Baptist to be baptized by him in order to fulfill all righteousness. When Jesus came out of the water, the Holy Spirit/Ghost came down from Heaven and alighted on Him. Jesus was no longer a mere man; His baptism empowered Him, authorized Him, and sanctioned Him by the Spirit of God. He was anointed to take His place in the mission God planned for the salvation of men before the world began.

After His baptism, The Holy Spirit lead Him into the desert to be tempted by Lucifer, with each temptation the devil presented to Him, Jesus answered, *"It is written, it is written it is written."* Jesus spent forty days and forty nights in the heat of the day and the cold of the night. The devil thought He (His flesh) would be weak because He hadn't eaten for forty days and forty nights. I believe Satan was a little cocky thinking He could persuade the Savior of the world to sin. After all, it worked with Adam in the Garden of Eden. When Jesus returned from the wilderness He went into the temple and announced…

> The Spirit of the Lord is upon Me, because He has anointed Me to preach the gospel to the poor; He has sent Me to heal the broken hearted, to proclaim liberty to the captives and recovery of sight to the blind, to set at liberty those who are oppressed; to proclaim the acceptable year of the Lord.
>
> – Luke 4:18-19

Jesus visited Isaiah in a vision around 920 BC and prophesied about the surrounding countries and of His ministry as the Christ. Nine hundred years later, Jesus, as a man filled with the Holy Spirit, went into the synagogue and read the passages He revealed to Isaiah beforehand about Himself to whosoever in the synagogue. When He finished reading, He closed the book, gave it to the attendant and sat down. This is awesome within itself, as God, He predicted, forecast, and foretold the actions He would accomplish a thousand years later as a man filled with God. In the synagogue all eyes were on Him when He said, ***"Today this Scripture is fulfilled***

God's Blueprint

in your hearing." Then Jesus went to Capernaum, a city of Galilee where He taught and did what God told Him to teach and do, so He cast out unclean spirits, healed Peter's mother-in-law who was sick with high fever, and when the sun was setting He healed all those who were brought to Him who were sick and those with various diseases. He laid His hands on them and healed them all. Demons also came out of many people crying out and saying, "You are the Christ, the Son of God." But Jesus rebuked them and did not allow them to speak for the demons knew He was the Christ.

Jesus said God *anointed* Him to preach the Gospel. In order to be anointed, God must impart the Holy Spirit to the person who has been ordained to take an office for His Kingdom. God anointed Jesus to preach and when Jesus preached, or said what God said; the power of the Word changed the lives of all who believed. So the people who believed in Him as the Son of God had their lives changed from death to life. For those who did not believe, their lives also changed but it was from natural death to eternal death. Every one dies once and then judgment—unbelievers are [already] judged through their belief system, their actions and deeds during their lifetime.

Jesus could not do this as a mere man; the power of

The Blueprint

the Holy Spirit had to come upon Him and empower Him to preach the Gospel, heal the sick and cast away devils and demons and raise the dead. We cannot do the work of the Gospel either, without the power of God on us.

God gave Jesus the command to:
- Preach to the poor.
- Heal the brokenhearted
- Proclaim liberty to the captives
- The recovery of sight to the blind
- To set at liberty those who are oppressed
- And to proclaim the acceptable year of the Lord.

Here is the Blueprint

For I have not spoken on My own authority; but the Father who sent Me gave Me a command, what I should say and what I should speak.
– John 13:49

Jesus did not come from Heaven to do His own thing. He did not empty Himself of power or make Himself of no reputation to see His Name in neon lights or crafty billboards; He came to help us see the light. He came by the command of God the Father to speak what He speaks and do what He does for the people

God's Blueprint

on Earth. It was God Who worked through Jesus to heal the sick, to raise the dead, to teach people about the Kingdom of God. It is important for us to know this because believers are commanded to do what Jesus did. Our ministries should parallel the ministry of Jesus because the same Holy Spirit that dwelt in Jesus also dwells in believers. Furthermore, believers have basically the same command that God gave His Son. The only difference is Christ died for our sins which paved the way for us to become functioning believers. *Our commission* is a spinoff of the commission of God to Jesus

For the first thirty years, Jesus did not do any miracles because He was a mere man. But when Jesus was baptized by John the Baptist, the Holy Spirit descended like a dove from Heaven and alighted upon Him when He came up from the river. Before, He did not do any miracles before the Spirit of God fell on Him. But after the Spirit of God came upon Him, He was equipped to do the miracles He was called to do. God's blueprint for Jesus was to say what the Father says, and to do what the Father does. So every time He preached the spoken Word, or the Rhema Word of God, or what the Father said, miracles happened and lives changed.

Jesus never sinned once, but the human race has a

The Blueprint

history of sin. Jesus did not have to repent of His sins because He never sinned. However, we were born sinners and needed to repent of our sins and also ask for the Lord to come in our lives. When we do this we are born again and The Holy Spirit literally comes into our lives as He came in the life of Christ. Now we are equipped to follow God's blueprint to speak what the Holy Spirit speaks and do what the Holy Spirit tells us to do. This is God's blueprint for the human race.

> Therefore, if any are in Christ, he is a new creation; old things have passed away behold all thing have become new. – 2 Corinthians 5:17

New does not mean we start over as human beings, it means our faith in Christ and His work on the cross creates a new life or a new mentality of Christ in us. He is no longer a mere thought in our minds; He is no longer just a mental assent or an idle notion. When the Holy Spirit entered into us we became *empowered* just as Christ was empowered. The same Holy Spirit that dwelt in Christ now dwells in us. Now our habits have changed, our conversation has changed, our goals have changed, and our entire lives have changed. We are no longer mere men and woman; we are children of God, filled with the Spirit of God.

God's Blueprint

■ ■ ■

Our ministries should parallel the ministry of Jesus because the same Holy Spirit that dwelt in Jesus also dwells in believers.

Some believers think Jesus was God for His entire earthly life and He was; He just didn't possess the power of God through the first thirty years. If Jesus had the power of God during His first thirty years as a man, why would God the Holy Spirit have to come upon Him at His baptismal? Why would God the Son need the power of God, if He was already equipped with the power of God? Remember, He emptied Himself of Himself to born of a woman. He made Himself of no reputation to become a servant to mankind. The Word was made flesh and dwelt among men.

Jesus gave believers the command to:

All authority has been given to Me in heaven and on earth. Go therefore and make disciples of all nations, baptizing them in the name of the Father and of the Son and of the Holy Spirit, teaching them to observe all things I have commanded you, and lo, I am with you always, even to the end of the age. – Matthew 28:18

Jesus received all the authority again. He was no

The Blueprint

longer a mere man but was reestablished as the Son of God in power, majesty and wisdom. He was back to Himself and took His rightful place at the right hand of God.

But before He ascended, He gave His followers the commands for all believers, it is the blueprint for Kingdom living in accordance to God's plan for mankind. We are to *make disciples of all nations.* We are to be a witness for Jesus and tell how He changed our lives. We are to give testimony of how we lived in spiritual poverty and how Jesus brought us into His Kingdom as children of God. We are to baptize all those who come in the Name of The Father, The Son and the Holy Spirit. We are not to sprinkle those who are being baptized; we must *submerge* them under the water because it *represents* the death, burial and resurrection of Jesus Christ. When we are baptized, we are identified with Jesus on His burial and His resurrection. We are to teach believers all things that Jesus taught us through His Word and He promised that He would be with us until the end of the age.

Go into the world and preach the gospel to every creature, He who believes and is baptized will be saved; but those who does not believe will be condemned. And these signs will follow those who believe: In My name they will cast out demons, they will speak with new tongues; they will take up serpents and if they drink anything deadly; it will by no means hurt them; they will lay hands on the sick, and they will recover."

– Mark 16:15-18

This is known as **The Great Commission** and it is very similar to God's commission to Jesus. God's commission to Jesus was to:

1. Preach to the poor.

2. Heal the broken hearted

3. Proclaim liberty to the captives.

4. The recovery of sight to the blind and to

5. To set at liberty those who are oppressed and to proclaim the acceptable year of the Lord.

Jesus' commission to the disciples and the Church according to Mark:

1. Preach the Gospel

2. He who believes is baptized

3. Cast out demons

4. Speak with new tongues

5. Lay hands on the sick and they will recover

The Blueprint

Jesus' commission to the Church according to Matthew:

1. Teach the Gospel to every creature

2. Make disciples of all nations

3. Baptize them in the Name of God the Father, God the Son and God the Holy Ghost

4. Teaching all things Jesus commanded

5. And Jesus will be with us until the end of the age.

All the work of the Gospel, the miracles, the teachings, the preaching, and the demonstrations of the power of God had come to a climax, to the point where Jesus prepared the disciples to take up the ministry where He left off.

Again, Jesus could not do this as a mere man; the power of the Holy Spirit had to come upon Him and empower Him to heal the sick and cast out devils and demons. Again, we cannot do the work of the Gospel either without being born again, with the power of the Holy Spirit working through us. So we must heed to the Voice and the leading of the Holy Spirit as Jesus heeded to the Voice of the True and Living God.

Mark's version of the Great Commission gives us a

God's Blueprint

little more detail. Every person on the planet must hear the Gospel of Jesus, He must be preached to the ends of the earth, in the cities, in jungles, at both of the polar caps and all in between. He must be preached in the East, out West, up North and down South. Every individual who hears this Gospel of life must make up their minds about THE TRUTH OF JESUS before He comes back for His people— believers. Everyone who believes the Gospel and is baptized will be saved, but everyone that does not believe will be condemned or renounced.

These aren't suggestions; these two collections of Scriptures are divine commands or orders for each individual that believes in Christ Jesus as Lord. God gave Jesus commands and He completed the tasks God intended. Jesus gave His Church commands and He expects these tasks to be done also. Jesus did not give us task to do without the blueprint.

The Blueprint for Believers

For I have not spoken on My authority; but the Father who sent Me gave Me a command, what I should say and what I should speak. And I know that His command is everlasting life. Therefore, what I speak, just as the Father has told Me, so I speak. – John 12:49-50

The Blueprint

This is what separates the truth from the false. This is what separates us from victory and defeat. This is what separates us from being giants in the Kingdom of God or jellyback Christians stuck in *traditions of men*. When we speak on Gods authority, His will shall be done. When we speak on our own authority, we will eventually devolve as a false prophet, because our pride issues keep us in disobedience to the blueprint.

The blueprint for successful Christian living and ministry is speak what Jesus speaks and do what Jesus did. Christians! It is a must that we follow the blueprint Jesus followed when He was a man on Earth empowered by The Holy Spirit. Remember He made Himself of no reputation, laid down His eternal power; He emptied Himself of Himself and became a man, or became flesh. And God the Father worked miracles through God the Son. He healed people through God the Son. He delivered people through God the Son. All the miracles, all the signs and all the wonders, and all the teachings that Jesus taught while on Earth, was done by the Father working through Him.

We as believers cannot do any work of God unless the Holy Spirit works through us. *(As the Spirit wills.... See: 1 Corinthians 12:11)* As God worked through Jesus back in the day to minister to this lost and dying world; the Holy Spirit works through believers

God's Blueprint

today because it is still a lost and dying world. The Holy Spirit that worked through Jesus, is the same Holy Spirit that works through believers.

There are times in our lives we want to go somewhere and do the Lord's work. We want to preach the Word and cause ten thousand men and women to come to the Lord. Sometimes we want to go to Africa and preach the Gospel, or South America to lay hands on the sick. I know of two sisters from England who went to Africa to minister but they died because they just went. They just decided to go without the leading of the Holy Spirit. I guess they did not know the Holy Spirit goes before us to prepare the hearts of men and women for God. If they waited for the Holy Spirit to set the atmosphere in place, the girls would have been successful. I want you to know there are good ideas and God ideas. The girls had a good idea about going to Africa and helping the natives spiritually just as Paul wanted to go to Asia and Bithynia but the Spirit would not let him. We need to recognize the prompting of the Holy Spirit, and know the difference between good and God ideas.

Note: We cannot just run around trying to do the work of God on our own. We have to follow the lead of the Holy Spirit. An example is Acts 16 where Paul wanted to go to Asia to preach the Word, but

The Blueprint

the Spirit would not let them. They wanted to go to Bithynia but the Spirit did not permit them to do so. So they traveled on until Paul had a vision of a man in Macedonia. Paul concluded this is where The Holy Spirit wanted them to go. There was a need there. When Paul and his party arrived, a woman named Lydia and her family were baptized, a slave girl was delivered from witchcraft or divination. This girl followed Paul's group proclaiming, "They were servants of the Most High God, who proclaim the way of salvation." Paul was irritated by the slave girl because she wasn't genuine. She was under the influence of Satan, proclaiming *the way* of salvation. So Paul cast the evil spirit out of her.

Because of this, her master was irate with Paul and Silas since the slave girl was now useless and couldn't use the craft of divination any longer. This meant their fortune-telling business would dry up and die. The master of the girl was greatly annoyed and stirred up the city proclaiming Paul and Silas were teaching a God they didn't know or care for because He was contrary to their own demonic way of life. So they were severely beaten and thrown into prison; even worse, the inner prison.

Even though they were beaten and treated badly, the *obedience* of Paul and Silas to the Holy Spirit saved

God's Blueprint

lives and it is an example of God's blueprint in action, that came with results. The Holy Spirit told them where to go and they went, they baptized a family, they cast out a demon, and they went to jail. While they were in jail, they counted it all joy, praising the Lord and the prisoners heard them. This means that even though they were in jail, they were not prisoners. You can be free even in prison. Paul and Silas may have been locked up, but they were free to praise God, free to worship Him and free to glorify His Name. And the bound prisoners heard them. Then the earth shook, the doors of the jail flew open, but no one escaped. Generally when prison doors swing open, prisoners will become track stars. But something *extraordinary* happened, and it had their attention. The jailer was about to commit suicide because he saw the open doors and assumed the prisoners escaped. In those days, when a prisoner escaped from jail or any type of custody, the prison guard in charge would inherit their sentences. If the escaped prisoner had a twenty year sentence the guard would have to finish his twenty years sentence. So as the guard was about to kill himself, Paul told him to stop, no one had ran off. So the guard took Paul and Silas to his house and bandaged their wounds and asked a question every believer wants to hear, "How can I get saved?" So the guard and his family were saved by the blood of the Lamb that night. The only reason

The Blueprint

Paul and Silas had victory is because they were obedient to the Holy Spirit.

■ ■ ■

Now we are equipped to follow God's blueprint to speak what the Holy Spirit speaks and do what the Holy Spirit tells us to do. This is God's blueprint for the human race.

When we repent of our sins and ask Jesus to be our Lord and Savior, the Holy Spirit will come down on us. He may not come as a floating dove and alighting on you as He did with Jesus. He may not come as a mighty rushing wind with *tongues of fire* as He did on *[the Day of Pentecost]*. I didn't see any of that when I was born again, but I was overwhelmed with the power of the Holy Spirit when I confessed my sins and asked Jesus into my life. For the first four or five days I barely ate anything or left my room because I was only hungry for the Word of God, praying in the Spirit and reading Matthew, Mark, Luke, and John at least twelve hours a day, every day. The Holy Ghost was actually training me in the Word, revealing Jesus to me by the Word, and guiding me as I immersed myself in the Word of God and prayer. I lost all my old friends, but I gained new friends that are like-minded. But the best

God's Blueprint

friend of all is Jesus the Christ—I was born again. I was no longer blind and ignorant to the Word of God, I was no longer a citizen of the world, because the Holy Ghost gave me clarity and I began understanding the Scriptures. I was no longer a slave to sin but alive to Christ because *the nature of God* was now in me.

In the Old Testament, God only anointed Kings, Priests and Prophets to complete specific tasks He desired. As you know *the anointing* is an impartation of the Holy Spirit to men and women to complete a task for the Kingdom of God. Today, all true believers are anointed in one area or another. Many are anointed as Pastors, Teachers, Bishops, Evangelist, Apostles, singers, and psalmist in whom the Holy Spirit leads and guides to say what God says and to do what God does. This impartation is not limited to Pastors, Teachers, Bishops, Evangelist, Apostles, singers and psalmist – the impartation is for all believers on every level who believe in Jesus and live by the Spirit of God.

> Most assuredly, I say to you, the Son can do nothing of Himself, but what He sees the Father do; for whatever He does, the Son also does in like manner. – John 5:19

According to Jesus Himself, He could not initiate any works of His own. *"The Son cannot do anything in*

84

The Blueprint

Himself." Jesus could only do what He saw His Father do; like Father, like Son. Likewise, believers cannot do anything of ourselves so we must be sensitive and rely on the Holy Spirit so we can say what He says and do what He does through the Holy Spirit.

> I have not spoken on My own authority; but the Father who sent Me gave Me a command, what I should do and what I should speak. And I know that His command is everlasting life. Therefore, whatever I speak, just as the Father told Me, so I speak. – John 12:29

Jesus said only what the Father said and worked what He witnessed His Father work. So the key to a successful life in Christ and in ministry is to never speak on our own authority or in our own strength. We must speak and do as Jesus spoke and did. When Jesus ascended into Heaven, He sent the Holy Spirit to the men and women in Christ to teach us and guide us and to show us things to come. When Jesus' earthly ministry came to an end, fifty days later, the visible ministry of the Holy Ghost began. *The Book of Acts* is the perfect example for us in the works of the Holy Spirit. The Apostles did the same miracles Jesus did; they healed the sick and raised the dead just as Jesus did. They taught what Jesus taught and lived as Jesus lived.

God's Blueprint

There are many denominational Christians who do not believe they can fulfill this particular Scripture for whatever reason. One of the reasons may be the, "I'm not worthy" clause! We see Jesus as the greatest man that ever lived and then compare Him to ourselves. We believe our feet cannot fill the sandals of Jesus and then create a low spiritual self-esteem with the vocabulary of 'can't' and 'unworthy' and 'won't work'. But Jesus said we can do these miracles if we believe what He says about us. We are to take our faith to the next level daily and believe what Jesus says. We obviously believe He saved us from death, Hell, and the grave. We obviously believe He gave us eternal life. We obviously believe He walked on water; as did Peter. So why can't we obviously do the works of Christ through prayer and the stewardship of the Holy Spirit? One answer is because of unbelief, and the other is practicing sin in our lives, or living in the flesh.

Note: There is a big difference between being a believer and being an unbeliever in the Church. Believers are cheerful and happy most any time. They're full of love, having fallen in love with the Word of God; on the other hand, unbelievers in the Church are always non-chalant, always wondering, but never initiating a desire to look into THE TRUTH.

The Blueprint

■ ■ ■

... the anointing is an impartation of the Holy Spirit to men and women to complete a task for the Kingdom of God.

Faith comes by hearing and hearing by the Word of God. If our faith is weak—we need to strengthen it by hearing from God. We need to soak ourselves in Matthew, Mark, Luke and John. The more we read, the more faith we obtain. The more we hear about the Bible, about God, about Jesus, about the Holy Spirit, the stronger our faith becomes. Our job is to believe God no matter what. God is TRUTH and His Word is TRUTH. We need to envision ourselves doing the works of Jesus. We need to pair it up in the Scriptures and see it in our imagination. Remember, we walk by faith and not by sight.

This example is not just for Jesus or the Apostles alone, but for Believers today. God's Word is everlasting and eternal, what Jesus said two-thousand years ago is applicable today and appropriate today. His Word is still pertinent, it remains valid and it is relevant today for the Body of believers (His Church), where Jesus is the Head. So we know the Church today can do the works that Jesus did, if only we believe. So just as Jesus listened to the Fa-

God's Blueprint

ther, we must listen to the Holy Spirit, Whom the Father sent to us to do greater works for His Kingdom. We can honestly walk as Jesus walked when we believe and abide in Him. This is the Blueprint for believers.

Chapter 8
TO WALK AS HE WALKED

Most assuredly, I say to you, he who believes in Me, the works that I do he will do also; and greater works than these he will do, because I go to my Father.

– John 14:12

We will either believe this verse or not. *Believing* is the difference between eternal life and eternal damnation. Believing is the difference blessing and cursing. Jesus is the greatest person ever, (He came to Earth as a man), to walk this earth as a man; yet, when we read His teachings and hear about His works, we find them to be phenomenal, extraordinary, and exceptional. He says believers can do the same works He did if we believe. The word *'if'* is powerful two letter word and it can lead you to life or death; it depends on what side of 'if' you are on. Then He continues and says, ***"Greater works than these we will do because He was going to His Father."*** We need to walk as Jesus walked.

So, as Jesus was baptized in the Holy Spirit, we should

be baptized in the Holy Spirit. As Jesus healed the multitudes, we should be able to heal a multitude. As Jesus walked on water, we should be able to walk on water. As Jesus raised the dead, we should be able to raise the dead. As Jesus fed thousands with a small amount of food, we should be able to feed thousands the same way. We should be able to lay hands on those who have Cancer, AIDS, Diabetes, demons, devils, Hypertension, Alzheimer, Dementia, Ebola, Zika, broke arms and legs, and all other sicknesses, diseases and viruses and they will recover. (See: Mk 16:15) We need to know He gave us a *legal right* to become sons and daughters of God, because we believe. (See: Jo 1:12) When we operate our lives as legal sons and daughters of the Most High, we will be able to do all things the Holy Spirit tells us to do. We will have a boldness to say all things the Holy Spirit tells us to say.

Sometimes we judge ourselves in a negative light. Jesus says we can do the works He did, but we can't see ourselves fulfilling this particular Scripture. We may have cussed, or looked at the attributes of a beautiful woman or a handsome man too long, or lied about something earlier that day or last week and don't feel worthy or valuable of fulfilling this Scripture. Some just feel unworthy; while others believe they cannot achieve this because their minds are in the flesh. I've crossed paths with some that believe this statement is ludicrous and don't believe what Jesus told us to do. If so, that would make them a non-believer. Now, you can believe that Jesus came from Heaven to save us from our sins. You believe in all the works of Jesus. You believe that when we pass away we're Heaven bound. How is it we don't have the faith to do the works Jesus told us to do? Most of this is the result of a lack of faith in Christ, poor teaching or *sugar coated* messages spawned from fear of failure, but when we believe we will operate as the Spirit wills and Jesus will be exalted, glorified and praised.

> But he answered and said, "It is written, Man shall not live by bread alone, but by every word that proceeds out of the mouth of God. – Matthew 4:4

■ ■ ■

If our faith is weak—we need to strengthen it by hearing from God. We need to soak ourselves in Matthew, Mark, Luke and John. The more we read, the more faith we obtain.

As believers, we must take heed, pay attention, and concentrate on every Word that proceeds from the mouth of God. The Bible is the Word of God. Jesus set the example for us and His life is the blueprint for our life and ministry. When we do as Jesus did, and say what Jesus said, and wait on the Holy Spirit to guide us, we will be in a position to fulfill any and every Scripture God intends for us to accomplish as planned before the foundation of the world. When we take the Word of God straight up, not adding our feelings to it, or what we want it to say, or create ideas and traditions through selfish ambition or false interpretation then we'll be all right. But if we don't believe then we've created another god, another 'Jesus', another spirit and our life changes to being a success in failure.

The very first thing we must believe is:

1. Jesus is the Christ.

There are millions and billions of people who believe in Jesus as an ordinary man who had great talents. They believed He was a Prophet, a great healer, and an all around good guy but nothing more. Jesus was/is extremely more than that. We must believe He is the Anointed One, our Salvation, and our rightful passage to Eternal Life.

2. We must believe in Jesus as the Son of God.

We must believe that Jesus was born of God in the spiritual realm and not created. We must believe God sent Him from Heaven to the earth to cleanse us from our sins and offer salvation to this lost and dying people of the earth. We must believe the earthly Jesus was born of Mary and was spoken into existence through the Holy Spirit, so that flesh would not be involved with the conception and birth of Jesus, (Mary was the only human being involved in the birth of Christ). We must believe Jesus lived His whole life without sin.

3. We must believe what the Bible teaches.

We must believe everything the Bible teaches specifically about Jesus, because it was Jesus that changed our lives. The Bible teaches that Jesus holds this planet and everything on this planet together in His power. The Bible teaches us that Jesus chose us to be *sons and daughters of God* before the creation of the heavens and the earth. The Bible teaches us that whosoever believes in Him will have everlasting life.

4. We cannot put God in a box.

There are millions of people who put God in a box saying and believing He doesn't heal anymore, or He doesn't perform miracles anymore, or He doesn't raise the dead anymore. People believe the power of God dwelling in people like the Apostles stopped in the first century. People act like God is dead but this statement is a lie and a million miles from the truth.

God's Blueprint

So when you put God in a box you will find yourself in a box because there are times when God will *allow* you to believe whatever you want to believe.

Chapter 9
PRAYER

Communication is a powerful tool in our relationship with God. In fact, we need to pray more than we eat. Every believer must practice, utilize, employ, develop and make use of prayer daily. In *prayer* we simply talk with God. We also praise Him for what He has done for us in the past. We worship Him because He is the True and Living God. We glorify His Name because He deserves it, and yes, we can make request.

> And whatever you ask in My name, that I will do, that My Father may be glorified in the Son. If you ask anything in My name, I will do it.
> – John 14:13-14

Whatever we ask in the Name of Jesus, will be done because Jesus said He will do it. Point Blank! The reason for answered prayer is that God may be glorified in the Son. There are people who prayed in this manner and received the answer to their prayers while others do not. Jesus will not answer selfish prayers, covetous prayers or greedy prayers. He will not answer any prayers filled with doubt and unbelief. He will however, answer prayers from our hearts when we pray in faith according to His Word, according to His plan for mankind.

> Is anyone among you sick? Let him call for the elders of the church and let them pray over him, anointing him with oil in the name of the Lord. And the Prayer of Faith will save the sick, and the Lord will raise him up, and if he has committed any sins, he will be forgiven. – James 5:14

■ ■ ■

Jesus set the example for us and His life is the blueprint for our ministry and life.

When a believer gets sick, he should call for the Elders of the Church. The *initiative* begins with the one who is sick. He should call for the Elders, and they will come lay hands on the sick, so that—they should recover. The Elders of the Church should meet the qualifications set in 1 Timothy 31-7, and Titus 1:5-9. *Elders* does not mean "old men," the Elders have the qualities of uprightness, *spiritual maturity*, and live in God's moral character. These Elders should be full of faith and ready to embrace or put into action any of the gifts of the Holy Spirit. As Overseers, these men hold positions of authority as prayer warriors and men of faith and power.

The oil is not a magic potion, but it is symbolic of the consecration and the joy in the presence of the Holy Spirit. There are some who say the oil is a representative of the Holy Spirit. The oil should be prayed over by the elders and allow God to bless it. So the results of this are (1) his sins are forgiven and (2) Jesus will raise him up.

> Jesus says, "Whatever you ask in My Name, that I will do." – John 14:13a

'Whatever', is a grammatical word used to refer to everything of a particular type, without limitation. There are *no limits* in Christ Jesus; there are no restrictions or confines in the Word of God. This is a strong statement from the King of kings and the Lord of lords and I have found it true. Whatever we ask from the Son of God, He will do it and we will receive it. We live by faith and not by maybe.

> ...that My Father may be glorified in the Son. If you ask anything in My name, I will do it.
> – John 14:13b-14

God's Blueprint

In the Strong's Exhaustive Concordance, the word *'glorify'* is to: render or esteem glorious, and full of honor. Glory is praise and thanksgiving offered as acts of worship to a deity, in this case—The True and Living God. To *give God the glory*, is to proclaim His magnificence, His grandeur, His brilliance, and His everlasting wonder. The more glory we give to God, the more God trust us.

So whatever we ask in the Name of Jesus, He will do, so that God the Father will be praised with thanksgiving as our act of worship. When we ask Jesus for anything, He will do it so that Jehovah will get the praise, glory, and honor He deserves.

The chart below will help us in our receiving of answered prayer:

- **Ask God**   Line it up with the promise of God.

                      This requires you to search the Bible for His promise for all believers. The promises of God are yes and amen.

- **Believe God**   Meditate on the request over and over in your mind.

Prayer

- **Receive from God**   Embrace the promise with your imagination over and over and expect it to manifest in your life.

- **Praise God**   Knowing that your prayer will be answered. This is not a hope He will, it is I know He will according to His Word.

- **Thank God**   For God will answer through faith and assurance.

God's Blueprint

Chapter 10

ONE

As Jesus conducted His earthly ministry, He was flesh and bone and could only be at one place at a time. He was much like us as far as mobility is concerned. He traveled on foot and sometimes on a donkey (which was the Cadillac of the day). Now if God wanted, He could have translated Jesus as He did with Philip in Acts 8, but He did not. Even though He did all those wonderful miracles, He could only be at one place at a time.

> Nevertheless, I tell you the truth. It is to your advantage that I go away; for if I do not go away, the Helper will not come to you; but if I depart, I will send Him to you. – John 16:7

The ministry of Jesus was a man filled with the Spirit of God teaching and preaching the Gospel wherever He went. When Jesus left the earth to go back to God, He sent the Holy Spirit to the believers on *the Day of Pentecost* to enable them to preach and teach the Gospel wherever they went. As far as mobility goes, The Holy Spirit is not limited as Jesus was in His earthly ministry. The Holy Spirit is *omnipresent, omnipotent* and *omniscient* and without any boundaries; whereas, Jesus had boundaries. Although filled with the Holy Spirit, He was a man enclosed in a skin suit. The Holy Spirit dwells in believers who are called to take up the ministry where Jesus left off. Instead of eleven born again disciples, there are millions of born again believers around the world with the ability to do what Jesus did. So these are the greater works Jesus told us about, every believer can do what Jesus did. This is not just the quality of work in the ministry but also the quantity of work in the ministry. The quality will always be holy, but the quantity will be thousands and millions of born-again believers doing the works of Christ.

■ ■ ■

When we ask Jesus for anything, He will do it so that Jehovah will get the praise, glory, and honor He deserves.

Jesus was not speaking to one person in this passage in John. He was speaking to a group of men who were going to be joined spiritually with Him and the Father through the Holy Spirit. It is not going to be one man doing the greater works but a collection of men filled with the Holy Spirit raising the dead, healing the sick all over the world.

The most wonderful benefit to being a born again believer is that we are now joined together with God; we are one with God the Father, and we are One in God the Son and we are One with the Holy Spirit. God is One with Us, God the Son is One with us and God the Holy Spirit is One with us; we are One in Him.

> Do you not know that you are the temple of God and that the Spirit of God dwells in you.
> – 1 Corinthians 3:16

The bodies of individual believers are actually individual Temples of God, or the true House of God. The Holy Spirit dwells in our bodies, which make us mobile Temples of God. As a mobile Temple of God, the Holy Spirit leads us everywhere we need to go. As mobile temples we are able to meet the needs of the people everywhere the Holy Spirit leads us to change the lives of others, just as our lives have been changed. This is part of *the Great Commission*, to change lives by preaching and teaching His Word. Now the local building where believers gather for praise, worship and whatever "thus says the Lord" is identified as God's Temple. But because of the indwelling of

God's Blueprint

the Holy Spirit in individual believers, His presence within us makes our bodies the Temple of God also.

> Now therefore, you are no longer strangers and foreigners, but fellow citizens with the saints and members of the household of God, having been built on the foundation of the apostles and prophets, Jesus Christ Himself being the cornerstone, in whom the whole building being fitted together, grows into a holy temple in the Lord, in whom you also are being build together for a dwelling place of God in the Spirit.
> – Ephesians 2:19-22

We are *no longer* strangers, foreigners, aliens, and outsiders to the Kingdom of God. We are no longer criminals, crooks, and sin practitioners; but we are fellow citizens, saints and members of the household of God. The Holy Spirit gave dictation to the Apostles and Prophets of old but Jesus the Christ brought it all together through His sinless life, His death, burial and resurrection. Believers are being fitted and built together through the training by the Holy Spirit into the dwelling place for the Spirit of God.

As we grow in the Spirit of God, we will endure problems, obstacles, difficulties, and impediments but the Lord will bring us through them all. Sometimes God will place a problem in our path but it is not for us to be overcome by the problem, nor to be defeated by the problem. Sometimes we will go through a *pruning* process in order to rid ourselves of questionable behavior or habits so that we may bear more fruit. *(cf. Jo 15:2)* This will be God molding us and shaping us into His image as powerful men and women of ministry and life. The reason for this is to strengthen us so that we will be *strong in the Lord and in the power of His might.*

Shortly before Jesus gave is life for us, He prayed to the Father for Himself, then He prayed for the disciples, and finally He prayed for those who would believe in Him through the witnesses of the disciples.

> I do not pray for these alone, (the eleven disciples), but for those who will believe in Me through their word; that they all may be One, as You Father are in Me, and I in You; that they also may be one in Us, that the world may believe that You sent Me. – John 17:20-22

It is a beautiful thing when the Creator of the universe prays for you thousands of years before you were born. When Jesus prays to the Father, you can best believe the prayer will come to pass. God the

God's Blueprint

Father will not deny the prayers of God the Son, He cannot deny Himself, because they are One and now we are *One* because we believe in Christ.

It's a privilege to be One in God, as God is One with you. To be One in Christ as Christ is One with you. To be One in the Holy Spirit as the Holy Spirit is One with us. I believe this is one of the greatest gifts given by the True and Living God. We need to wrap our minds around these Scriptures, and meditate on them day and night until they become reality in our lives. Then we will eventually fulfill the Scriptures as Jesus intends for us to do.

> In Him, we live and move and have our being.
> – Acts 17:28

When we realize we are One in Christ, our lives become more meaningful as we grow in the knowledge of Him. We will realize that He has been with us throughout our lives during the good and the bad seasons of our lives. Now that we are born again, He is closer to us because we are in Him.

> For we are His workmanship, created in Christ Jesus for good works which God had prepared beforehand that we should walk in them.
> – Ephesians 2:10

One

The genius of God's *new creation* work in each believer is that He renovates the nature of His redeemed children to make their good works a reality. God has a plan for each one of His children, but His plan could not be completed in the flesh, but by His Spirit dwelling in His children.

> There is therefore now no condemnation to them which are in Christ. – Romans 8:1

For all the men and women in Christ—there is no condemnation, no disapproval, no criticism, and no conviction for those who are in Christ. Through His indwelt presence, the Holy Spirit has in effect, brought the very life of Jesus Christ into our mortal bodies. As we yield ourselves to Him, Jesus becomes in and through us the fulfillment of the Word of God.

> I am the Vine and you are the branches,
> – John 15:5

Jesus is our *source* and we are the recipients of all that Jesus is. Jesus is our source and He is connected to us by living inside us by His Spirit. God the Father, God the Son and God the Holy Spirit are One. The Holy Spirit is the very energy of the believer's life. He maximizes our prayers and worship; He ministers through the Lord's Supper, and He enables us to continually draw our lives from Him.

Here is a note of warning. There will be naysayers around who will try and talk you down from something they do not understand. Most Christians are happy to be saved and nothing more. Unfortunately there are a lot of church goers who simply do not have an understanding of the dwelling place, the home for the Holy Spirit. When revelation of Christ is taught or preached, a lot of people will not plug in to who we are in Christ, our benefits in Christ, our position as children of God. Most of the time when people do not understand the ability to be sinless because God the Father and Jesus dwell in you through the Holy Spirit's indwelling presence; or that you are now dwelling inside the Trinity—they will just not get it. These folks mainly want to hear feel-good messages about the heroes of old instead of revelations of who we are in Christ today. They will come against you as they did with Jesus and form a clique of likeminded people which is always trouble. Get rid of them. A house divided cannot grow, produce, develop, or mature. The only thing a house divided can do is fall.

The most wonderful benefit to being a born again believer is that we are now One in God, we are One

One

in God the Son and One with the Holy Spirit. God is One with Us, God the Son is One with us and God the Holy Spirit is One with us.

He who says he abides in Him ought himself also to walk just as He walked. – 1 John 2:6

God's Blueprint

Chapter 11

OUR SPIRITUAL STATE

I write to you, little children, because your sins are forgiven you for His name sake. I write to you fathers, because you have known Hiim who is from the beginning. I write to you young men, because you have overcome the wicked one. I write to you little children, because you have known the Father. I have written to you fathers, because you have known Him who is from the beginning. I have written to you young men, because you are strong, and the word of God abides in you. And you have overcome the wicked one.

– First John 2:12-14 NKJV

Our spiritual status differs from person to person. One person may read the Bible and pray, (commune with God), all day long and just enjoy His presence. The more we commune with God, the stronger we become spiritually. There are those that gave their lives to Christ years ago and are mature in the Word. Then there are those who are young in the Lord, but they've *experienced* or witnessed the work of Christ.

God's Blueprint

John addresses different groups of believers in the Church. These age groups are not according to their physical age, but according to their levels of spiritual growth. The Apostle's purpose is to encourage believers to continue to grow in the Lord and to warn them of *temptations* that are coming for each believer.

■ ■ ■

The more we commune with God, the stronger we become spiritually.

These verses above describe two sets of encouragement to three levels in the spirit of John's readers. John writes to the children of the Church because their sins are forgiven for the Namesake of Christ, and because they know Jehovah the father.

John writes to the fathers of the Church who have known Him and served Him from a young age. When they heard the message of salvation, they received it and have been walking and living out God's plan for their lives.

John writes to the young men because they have overcome the wicked one or the evil one. When the Word of God abides, dwells, or lives in you, you will be a strong and wise person in Christ. The wicked one cannot do anything to you because you are no longer spiritually ignorant but spiritually sound—however, that will not stop him from coming. But we know his tactics and warfare and we are well able (equipped) to see him coming.

God's Blueprint

Chapter 12
THE WORLD

Do not love the world or the things in the world. If anyone loves the world, the love of the Father is not in him. For all that is in the world – the lust of the flesh, the lust of the eyes and the pride of life – is not of the Father but is of the world. And the world is passing away, and the lust of it; but he who does the will of God abides forever. – First John 2:15-17 NKJV

The world, which literally means age, refers to a *godless system*. The world is a morally *evil system* opposed to all that God is and holds dear. Needless to say it's a *satanic system* that opposes, goes against, resists, and even fights against God's moral character and resists Christ's Kingdom on this earth. The world caters to all things Jesus created, but would rather worship the created things through the five senses of the flesh rather than serving God. What we *see, hear, smell, touch* and *taste* can have a tremendous effect on our lives if we cater, provide, or gratify, our wants and desires exclusively to the creation instead of the Creator.

God's Blueprint

When we do this, we are an enemy of God. The pull or power of this world is a strong, intense, extreme desire to bring personal satisfaction. Whatever will bring us pleasure through our five senses. This is the focus of the world.

God tells us, ***"Do not love the world or the things in the world."*** We are to worship God alone; the things He created should not supersede our worship to Jehovah. When we focus our heart's desire on material things, spend our time in focusing on self-gratification, and then we are living our lives in the world. When *self-focus* is our goal then the love of the Father is not in us. When we don't have the love of the Father, then we don't know Jesus. When we don't know Jesus then our lives will be full of crime, transgression, vices and failure.

The three weapons the world uses with great success is the lust of the eyes, lust of the flesh and the pride of life. The *lust of the eyes* is a desire for sinful sensual pleasures. The *lust of the flesh* refers to covetousness or materialism, and the *pride of life* is simply being proud about one's position in the world, or church or company or some organization; "King of the Hill."

The *world's system* is constantly attempting to

116

change the ways and events of the physical world. The earth is experiencing many calamities such as earthquakes, tsunamis, hurricanes on land and under the sea, and tornados. Death is everywhere and can come at anytime. People are losing their minds because they cannot reverse global climate changes. They have assembled meetings, conferences, seminars, and heavy discussions on how to stop global warming. The truth is we, as the people of this planet have not taken care of Earth as we should. I believe our spiritual status has a lot to do with the decaying of the earth. Because of *Adam's sin*, the ground was cursed for his sake. What was once good in the eyes of God is now cursed. Adam's disobedience to the one command of God cursed us. I believe this is a perpetual curse, a continuous curse, or a permanent curse because the world is passing away and all the lusts that is in it. In fact, in 2 Peter 3:10, Peter reveals that Heaven and Earth will pass away with a tremendous noise and the elements of the earth will melt in fervent heat. One of the elements of the earth is air. It is amazing to think that air and the oceans will melt, along with all the elements that make up the earth. Can you imagine that? But there is *Good News*, "He that does the will of God will live forever."

And do not be conformed to this world, but be

transformed by the renewing of your mind, that you may prove what is that good and acceptable and perfect will of God. – Romans 12:2

We are not to accept the pattern of an age whose god is Satan. On the contrary, we are to be transformed by a renewed mind committed to the ideals of the Kingdom of God. For us to prove this, is to practice godly living, so that God's will for us is good and acceptable and perfect.

■ ■ ■

When we focus our heart's desire on material things, spend our time in focusing on self-gratification, and then we are living our lives in the world.

We are in this world, but we are not of this world's system. We may be surrounded by the people of the world, but our interest is in the Kingdom of God. The world is forever training people of the earth on how and what to think on any given subject. Millions of people get out of their beds everyday and tune in to the media and join the activities of the world all day long, but don't realize they are being trained or *brainwashed* in the ideology, philosophy,

The World

beliefs, principles, ideas, and even the dogma of the world's system, (and become people who don't know Jesus.) There's a multitude of people that are so enslaved with the lust of the flesh, lust of the eyes and the pride of life that Jesus, the Son of God is pushed away and is not welcome in daily living. Believers are to be transformed, *converted*, or altered and the doctrine of Jesus which will manifest with our relationship with Jesus.

We, the Body of Christ should *renew our minds* by reading the Word of God daily, praying with God daily, giving thanks to Jesus daily, and being obedient to His Word, The Bible, daily. When we renew our minds in this manner, during every session we spend with God, we will eventually become strong in the Lord and in the power of His might. We will have the wisdom of God to see the traps of the world approaching even when they're miles away.

Be doers of the word; and not just hearers only, deceiving yourselves. For if anyone is a hearer of the word and not a doer, he is like a man observing his natural face in a mirror; for he observes himself, goes away and immediately forgets what kind of man he was. But he who looks into the perfect Law of Liberty and continues in it, and is not a forgetful hearer but a doer of the work, this one will be blessed in what he does. – James 1:21-25

If you are a hearer of the Word only and not a doer of the Word, you have wasted your time and you have deceived yourself. You're like a man that looks at his face in the mirror and when he turns around, he forgets what he looks like. That's a terrible thought. Hearers of the Word only are people with a short attention span. They go to church but can't focus on the preaching or teaching because their minds are on material things or football, or movies and a date with the girl on the second row. Then there are some who don't remember what the Pastor preached thirty minutes later. To hear the Word of God and to do nothing is a sign of a deceived heart. It is sad to say that hearers only are a part of the world's system because the world's screaming for their attention and it divides, and eventually overcomes the hearts of church goers.

Obedience to the Word of God brings about the work of God. We are to hear the Word of God and then do the work of God. When the Holy Spirit tells us to do something, like God told Jesus to do something, we'll be blessed and the lives of people we come in contact with will be blessed also. Faith acts for doers of the Word.

The World

Beloved, I beg you as sojourners and pilgrims, abstain from fleshly lust which war against the soul, having your conduct honorable among the Gentiles, that when they speak against you as evildoers, they may, by your good works which they observe, glorify God in the day of visitation.

— 1 Peter 2:11

First of all, we are just visitors here on the earth. We're actually paying rent on the earth and will never own it. Our life span varies in different locations of the earth; for instance the United States life span is 71.4 years, Sierra Leone's life expectancy is only 50.1 years and the highest is Japan with the life expectancy of 83.7 years. No matter how long we live, the Bible says our lives are like the morning dew that evaporates when the heat of the sun pours it rays on the earth. We're sojourners, visitors, or guests of the earth. So it is very important how we live, and we must be attentive with our lifestyle for our flesh is at the door waiting for us to step out of line regarding the Word of God. As mentioned before, this earth will melt into non-existence at the end of days.

Peter warns his congregation then and the believers of today to abstain, refrain, and desist from fleshly lusts which war against our souls. Even though Jesus cleansed us from our sins, the desires of the flesh make an appearance from time to time. One that's most noticeable is angry drivers on the roads and highways honking their horns, shaking their fist, or giving the middle finger to others, because they lack peace. Some drivers will shoot you if their judgment warrants it. So we must abstain from getting in the flesh to avoid getting into encounters with the citizens of the world, if we don't, we'll be a star in the episode of, "When two dummies meet."

The sexual revolution has ruined many people through the years and has made a strong push in these later days. Getting high is the number one agenda for a lot of people. Drugs and sex goes hand in hand like socks and shoes. Having sex with good looking or desirable people drives millions of people in their daily activities. They are *driven* to have sex with whosoever, every chance they get. Men and women go to clubs in an attempt to find a sex partner for the night, while others just take on different partners each and every day. Then there's sex for hire which some say is the oldest profession on the earth. Finally there are people who kidnap children to use as sex slaves. The flesh controls everyone in the world that does not know Jesus, and the flesh is a patient driver, relentlessly seeking to cause those in Christ to stumble.

Porn is very popular with the people of the world to-

The World

day and sexual desires can be strong with both men and women. Unfortunately, Pastors, Preachers, and Teachers of the Gospel have made themselves victims in the affects of watching porn. The devil influences illicit sex between men and women and the number is growing of same sex relationships.

We are sojourners, visitors, and pilgrims in this world. This earth is not our home; we're just passing through because we have a better home in Heaven with God, Jesus and all the saints that lived before us and after us. Where we go after death depends on how we lived. The choices we make while living in this dirt suit or flesh will determine where we will live after we die.

Because we abide in Christ, we have the ability to abstain from fleshly desires. That does not mean these desires won't come, because they will. Evil desires will try to persuade us to do evil each and every day. As Believers, we are armed with the indwelling of the Holy Spirit, or our new nature provided by Christ, and we'll be able to ward off the advances of the devil and his imps. Because of this, we can abstain from fleshly lust that war against us.

If the world hates you, you know that it hated Me before it hated you. If you were of the world, the world would love its own. Yet because you are not of the world, but I chose you out of the world, therefore the world hates you. – John 15:18-19

If the world hates you, then you are in good shape because you have been *identified* with Christ. The old school religious group hated Christ then and like-minded people of today still hate Him because they don't know Him. If the world loves you, then you're in trouble with God and it will be evident that you are living in the flesh and practicing sin. The world and the Church should not have anything in common.

But when you are hated by the world, you're in good character because you are walking in the newness of life. You read the Gospel and believe what it says. When you believe the Words of the Bible then you live it. After you have read the Word with understanding and you retain the Word in your heart, you are able to preach or teach the Gospel. When you live the Gospel, the world watches you and develops a dislike for you that will eventually turn into hatred toward you. Your lifestyle contradicts the world's way of thinking and living. You no longer agree with the politics of the world and will have no part in the ways of the world.

One example is some Preachers; Teachers, Bishops and even the Pope have strayed away from doctrine of Christ. One reason is they don't meet the requirements of Timothy and Titus to be leaders of the Church. A lot times there is a need to fill a position in the Church, so the board or a committee just thrust any kind of person in a position of authority. I know a man that was put into a position of authority because he had a certificate but he didn't have a relationship with Christ. This man was fired because he watched pornography in his office daily while attempting to meet the spiritual needs of his people. Then there are Pastors and Teachers and other church leaders that have an affinity, an attraction and magnetism to rape young boys and girls in the church where they should be teaching the Gospel. Instead of satisfying the spiritual needs of the children, there are satisfying their own fleshly needs. Then there are so-called pastors that require the women to abstain from wearing panties during the services while other leaders demand sex with woman in order to be members of their church. Then there are praise leaders and choir directors who are actually active in homosexual encounters inside the church and out; but the leadership won't fired them or sit them down because they fear the congregation will be upset with him/her. These praise and worship leaders don't have but a handful of old Negro spirituals, or country favorites, or beloved bluegrass songs. Most of these songs are littered, or plagued, with doubt, defeat and depression. There aren't any new revelations in these songs. These leaders obviously don't know their actions are an abomination unto the Lord or they just don't care.

■ ■ ■

If the world hates you, then you are in good shape because you have been identified with Christ.

For the name of God is blasphemed among the Gentiles because of you," – Romans 2:24

It is a terrible thing when the world influences the Church. Then someone who's interested in church will see these activities and just figure, "They're no better than me." They will talk about the church, but most likely never return. I believe some people don't really want to continue fellowship with the devil, but if they see the church as just another example of devilish activities [in the Name of God], then why go to church? Sadly, these people will miss out on the true gift of Christ, unless the Holy Spirit intercedes.

Another example is the subject of *abortion*. Everything around this subject is wrong. First of all, it is a sin to engage in sex without marriage. It is a sin to kill any person whether it is a fetus or child or a full grown adult. It's terrible all the way around. Yet there are a lot of women who live their lives with the motto, "I can play and don't have to pay!" Meaning she can have all the sex she wants, but when she becomes pregnant, she can have it aborted. It starts with sin and ends with sin. There are women who are raped by whosoever and become pregnant by this awful act. It is a sad situation, but the baby is still a human being no matter the father. God does not agree with the killing of human beings. Then there are churches and organizations that picket abortion clinics, and speak hateful things about the sinners involved in this sin. The calling of the believer is not to picket, but to pray. It is not the design of the Father to argue about fleshly topics but to teach and preach His Gospel.

Then there's the issue of *gun control*. Due to church shootings, school shootings, night club shootings, concert shootings, grocery store shootings, movie shootings, and shootings everywhere else around the globe, people of the world want to reform gun control. The problem is not the guns; the problem is the people who don't know Jesus with the guns. Jesus said there will be an escalation of violence in the last days and so it is. But the world mistakenly attempts to form committees, commissions, boards, and agencies to cut down on these violent acts when Jesus said these very acts were going to happen because the world has rejected Him as the Son of God, as the Deliverer, and as the Salvation from the world. These committees, commissions, boards, and agencies will not be successful in anything but making matters worse mainly because the doctrine of Jesus is not welcome in their meetings or in their lives. Shootings and killings and wars will escalate until the day Jesus comes back. Jesus tells us this in Matthew 24, so the believer's purpose hasn't changed in the middle of this crooked and debased situation. We are still to evangelize the world, make disciples, preach and teach Jesus, and pray for our enemies. If we agree with the world's way of doing things we will find ourselves fighting against God and His plans.

> Where do wars and fights come from among you? Do they not come from your desires for pleasures that war in your members? You lust and do not have. You murder and covet but cannot obtain. You fight and war. Yet you do not have because you ask. You ask and you do not receive, because you ask amiss, that you may spend it on your pleasures. Adulterers and adulteresses! Do you not know that friendship with the world is enmity with God? Whoever wants to be a friend of the world makes himself an en-

emy of God. Or do you think that the scripture says in vain, "The Spirit who dwells in us yearns jealously. – James 4:1-5

James, the younger brother of Jesus, exposes the activities in the minds of *carnal Christians*. "Where do wars and fights come from?" They come from within you; they come as a courtesy of the desires and pleasures of the world. The world constantly attempts to parade its anti-God ideas, thoughts and dreams to your mind and through your eyes daily. If you are not renewing your mind, then your thoughts will become *carnal* instead of spiritual. You will *lose control* of yourself and conduct yourself like you did before you met Jesus. Your desires will change from serving God into friendship with the world. If you desire the things of the world, then you will have some complications in your life.

This Epistle of James is written to the Church. These activities are not wholesome for the Church. Some pray to God for someone else's husband or wife or other property. Some will kill, steal, rob, lie, trick and murder for other people's property or their position in life. Some pray for riches, prosperity, wealth, power, influence, supremacy and clout in order to compete with the citizens of the world. God will not answer any of these prayers because they're praying amiss or missing the point in God's covenant, character, and His plan for your life.

A lusting, warring, fighting Christian has not enveloped his/her born again experience, or treated it lightly. Even though we are born again believers, it does not mean life will be hunky-dory. The world has engaged in a constant pull on our new belief system and makes daily attempts to pull us back in the devil's way of doing things, mainly through the flesh triggered by the lust of the eyes. If you accept the whispering influence of darkness, you will certainly be in trouble with God.

■ ■ ■

It is not the design of the Father to argue about fleshly topics but to teach and preach His Gospel.

If you are a lover of the world and spend more time with the things Jesus created instead of the Creator, then you've made yourself an enemy of God. If you have an unhealthy adulation, hero worship, or admiration for anyone except God—then you have made yourself an enemy of God. Life will not be well with you on Earth and you will miss out on Heaven unless you truly repent, confess you sin and ask for forgiveness.

The World

True faith is humble and humility which is the opposite of the proud selfishness and self-centered ambition. There are believers who have fallen into this trap, and even leadership has the ability to fall into the snare when they take their eyes off God and believe, "It's all about me!" Our faith is boastful in Christ and not ourselves. Self-centeredness is the essence, spirit or the core or the fundamental nature of *worldliness*. God is a jealous God and will not be shared with anyone or anything, especially the world's way of thinking and living.

Note: If you are a believer and you are packing a pistol for your defense, then you are relying on your gun instead of relying on God. If God wants to bring you home or just end your life, you can have a thousand guns, hand grenades, and rocket launchers which would be of no use. When God calls us home—that's it. There's nothing we can do to keep our lives here on this earth.

> Grace and peace be multiplied to you in the knowledge of God and of Jesus our Lord, as His divine power has given to us all things that pertain to life and godliness, through the knowledge of Him who called us by glory and virtue, by which have been given to us exceedingly great and precious promises, that through

God's Blueprint

these you may be partakers of the divine nature, having escaped corruption that is in the world through lust. – 2 Peter 1:2-4

Chapter 13

DECEPTIONS OF THE
LAST HOUR – ANTICHRIST

L ittle children, it is the last hour; and as you
have heard that the Antichrist is coming,
even now many antichrists have come,
by which we know that this is the last hour. They
went out from us, but they were not of us; for if
they had been of us, they would have continued
with us, but they went out that they might be
made manifest, that none of them were of us.
– First John 2:18-19 NKJV

We are definitely in the last hour, or the last days as
we know it. The fact is we've been living in the last
days since the birth of Christ and the proof is the perpetual fulfilling of prophecy in Matthew 24, Mark
13 and Luke 21 concerning the activities in the last
days. There are wars around the globe, nations fighting against nations and within nations, ethnic group
against ethnic group, famines, natural disasters, racism, hatred, idolatry, escalating crime rates, people

are hated for being Christian and some are murdered for having a relationship with Christ, many people are offended because of Christ, and many have betrayed their brother or sister in Christ.

Families have different opinions on Jesus; fathers and sisters may love Him while mothers and brother may hate Him. We witness these actions daily and it's only going to get worse. *Lawlessness* is growing out of proportion and people are taking lawlessness a step further with each passing day. People don't respect man's rules or God's commandments. There is a lack of love throughout the world today. In fact, if Jesus doesn't come back soon, as promised, the people on the earth will perish by destroying one another. It may seem farfetched right now, but it is the truth. The people described above are antichrists. This group of people hates Jesus and has rejected Him as the Son of God; the result is a debased mind which will lead to spiritual ignorance and violence.

Deception is the practice of deliberately influencing someone to believe a lie on any given subject. The deceptions of Satan through the millenniums have ruined an untold number of men and women through lies, and half-truths. Most of these deceptions are religious or flesh-based, sometimes the two are combined. Satan has influenced men and women into believing there is more than one God, or taught to give service to many gods, then there's the teaching of the false belief that there are many roads to Heaven, so we don't have to travel through life on the straight and narrow road. People are *twisting* the Word to meet their own requirements of the flesh. If it feels good, do it!

■ ■ ■

We are definitely in the last hour, or the last days as we know it.

The antichrist (or anti-Christ) of this world teaches God is good and He will not punish us for our sins because He loves us. Some believe the devil will sit on the left side of God in Heaven, while Jesus sits on the right hand of God. The art of *compromising* God's Word by antichrists has been damaging to the churches, the nations, and individuals and caused them to become spiritually retarded. These are some of the reasons the life of crime for many escalates daily.

The false teacher or false prophet is led by the flesh, seeking to obtain power or gain for himself from the ministry. Initially, his message may not be false, but his motivation in the ministry is *fleshly*. This way he appeals to other fleshly people in the Church, offering them some carnal or *soulish* satisfaction. He will ultimately introduce doctrine that is contrary to the truth. Every believer must use the Word of God to measure the words of anything that any preacher speaks, and if there is any variation, any imbalance or any difference, in what he taught, then it must be questioned. We as believers need to be sensitive to the prompting of the Holy Spirit in judging the true from the false in preaching and teaching. We are to judge only the message of the teaching or preaching because God will judge the Teacher, the Preacher, the Bishop, and even the Pope.

I was driving up the Broadway Extension one day, a highway that connects Edmond, to Oklahoma City, and I saw a billboard that declared Abraham, Moses, Mohammed and Jesus were of one faith, the sign read they were all Muslim. I'm afraid this advertisement will deceive many people who don't know Jesus. Some are willing to accept an Islamic Jesus rather than the Jewish Jesus just to fit in somewhere. But the damage is going to be devastating for those who buy into these falsehoods, these deceptions and the trickery of misidentifying Jesus as just another false prophet. I was approached by some Muslims in the early eighties when I was a spiritual imbecile, but I had enough sense to flee when I was asked to deny Jesus. I had a Muslim girlfriend a long time ago who was convinced that Jehovah and Allah are the same God. The wages of this belief system on Judgment Day is going to be devastating, demoralizing, and destructive for all who believe in Allah as God because this system is Satanic and a main part of the antichrist system.

The Pharisees and the Sadducees are the founding fathers, or puppets of the *antichrist system*. These were the first ones who openly defied, challenged and confronted Jesus during His earthly ministry. These antichrists were specifically against Jesus the Christ. They were non-believers who did not believe in Jesus as the Son of God. They did not believe Jesus came down from Heaven in the flesh to redeem us from the law of sin and death. They hated Jesus because He did extraordinary miracles in public, but did not go to their school and learn to be religious. They hated Him because Jesus healed people on the Sabbath, delivered people on the Sabbath, cleansed people of leprosy and every other foul disease on Sabbath days. He did all manner of good every day, but the Pharisees, the Sadducees, and the scribes hated Him for it. This made them antichrist(s).

Jesus, the Messiah brought a new way of life to the world and the Pharisees and Sadducees were nervous about it because He was attracting a crowd everywhere He went. Multitudes came to Him to get their needs met, and the Pharisees and Sadducees were nervous about losing their prestige, their audience and the money in the collection plate. They felt Jesus was breaking the rules/laws of the Old Testament and worse, calling Himself the Son of God was blasphemous to them. These antichrist groups had lived their entire lives in the traditions of men, compromising the Scriptures and elevating themselves as a hierarchy over all others, but they couldn't see THE TRUTH right in front of them. The teachings, the miracles and the compassion of Christ were killing their *cult-like* ministries. So their number one priority was to stop Jesus in any way they could. When a person or a group of people do not understand another person or group of people—they will often murder whoever they don't understand.

These religious groups tried to question Jesus but came up short. They sought signs from Him but only received the sign of Jonah. They wanted to kill Him, but they couldn't. They wanted to catch Him in traps, but they were not successful. They even set up a harlot in an attempt for Him to break the law, but didn't succeed. Whatever they tried, they failed.

In the first century, the antichrist system would accuse Christians of *heresy*, or an opinion or belief that contradicts established religious teachings, and put them to trial, find them guilty and have the Roman government execute them for heresy. These antichrist groups thought they were dong God a service in eliminating the so-called heretics, but they were wrong. In the last days, *the Harlot church* will also accuse Christians around the world of heresy, find us guilty and will use the One World Government to execute us.

> These things I have spoken to you that you should not be made to stumble. They will put you out of the synagogues; yes, the time is coming that whoever kills you will think he's doing God a service." – John 16:1-2

The antichrist system is alive and well today. It is still hell-bent on destroying or diluting the Body of Christ with church and synagogue shootings and scandals complemented with false doctrine. Church leadership has been influenced to preach a *watered down* gospel and rape the children under their care. This all comes from the devil and his team, of like-minded people who perform these wicked and horrible acts every day and night. The antichrist system takes steps every day to denounce, criticize, discredit, condemn, distort, and of course lie about the truth of Christ. They do all they can to induce, encourage, and stimulate participation in the lust of the flesh, (Listed in: Ga 5:19; Ro 1:28; and Re 21:8) which happens to be advertised by the many forms of universal media.

God's Blueprint

The antichrist has the world in tow and has its own people tied up in social media, television, and the fads of the day, the gossip of the hour, and taking care of their own. So the world has their like-minded members already scripted, trained, and brainwashed, and locked into the things of the world. However, their main purpose, their main function is to convert Christians to their system of hate and deception through compromising the Scriptures, or appealing to the flesh and desires of men and women. So members of antichrist infiltrate churches whenever they are open for service. They'll seek out babes in Christ, *lukewarm* Christians or unstable people to pollute their spirits with deceitfulness, pretense, and treachery and go the extra mile to secure their soul to the world. If the Pastor of this church is weak, spiritually slow, has no backbone, and afraid of confrontation, then his/her church will split and be unfruitful for the Lord. But if the Pastor is a true Shepherd, he will not allow any member of his congregation to fall prey to the antichrist system. The antichrist spirit cannot dwell under the anointing of Jesus Christ for the Gift of Discernment reveals their true intentions. So when the antichrist is not successful in one church, they will find another one to dilute, or convert, or distract or lure them into disobedience to God's Word. As a turtle steals the catch of fish from fisherman's stringer, the antichrist sys-

140

Deceptions of the Last Hour...

tem tries to steal members from the Body of Christ.

Another tactic used by antichrist since the beginning of the Age of Grace is sending killers into congregations in an attempt to dissuade them from serving Christ. This strategy has had some success through the years, but many more have stood up for Christ. The persecutions of Christians is not new.

• Peter and John were arrested for healing a lame man.

• Steven, (one of the seven) was stoned to death, because he was full of faith and power, and did great wonders and signs among the people.

• Andrew, (one of the twelve) and Peter's brother was crucified upside down. He lived three days on the cross preaching Christ Jesus as Son of God before he died.

• Bartholomew was beaten with rods, and suspended him upside down and skinned him alive and after all this, he still preached the Gospel and exhorted the people until the king finally cut his head off to shut him up.

• The Jews plotted to kill Paul because he preached Christ.

• King Herod persecuted the Church and killed James, John's brother, he wanted to kill Peter also, but an angel of the Lord freed him from prison.

- Paul and Silas were beaten and jailed for *casting out a demon* that possessed a woman practicing divination (witchcraft).

- Also Paul was beheaded for the Gospel of Christ.

This is all the work of the antichrist.

■ ■ ■

Deception is the practice of deliberately influencing someone to believe a lie on any given subject.

The antichrist system is not just a religious system; *the American Civil Liberties Union* and several other organizations have been active in tearing down laws based on God's Word in the name of equality and the Constitution of the United States of America. When we base our lives on feelings, or what is right in our own eyes instead of basing our lives on the Word of God, we have lost touch and will find ourselves Hell-bound.

But you have an anointing from the Holy One, and you know all things. I have not written to you because you do not know the truth, but be-

cause you know it, and that no lie is of the truth.
– 1 John 2:20

Brothers and sisters in Christ are *anointed by God.* We have an *impartation* of the Holy Spirit dwelling in us. Whatever God has called us to do, He anoints us with the ability to perform the talent He has given us to change the lives of lost people according to *the Great Commission.* If God anointed you to teach His Word, then you will be gifted to teach under the influence of the Holy Spirit. If God anointed you to preach His Word, then you will be anointed, or gifted, to preach under the influence of the Holy Spirit. Whatever gift we receive from God, He anoints us with the Holy Spirit to complete the task we were called to do. The anointing also protects believers against false teachers because the wisdom and discernment of God is also in *the anointing.*

An example; God anointed John the Apostle to write this book entitled First John. The content of this book was given directly from God through the Holy Spirit. In other words, John took dictation and direction from the Holy Spirit and wrote the Gospel of John, First John, Second John, Third John, and The Revelation of Jesus Christ. This is a prime example of God working through ordinary men to bring His extraordinary Word to His children. For those who listen and believe the Word of God will be blessed and rewarded with life, but those who do not believe will be rejected by Christ. For those who believe in the Word of God will be anointed by God; but those who do not believe in the Word of God will receive the world's traditions and falsehoods which leads to eternal damnation.

One of the earliest forms of deception in the second century is Gnosticism. *Gnosticism* is a word derived from the Greek word, 'gnosis' which means knowledge. Gnostics later taught salvation by *mental enlightenment* which comes only to the spiritual elite, the influential, a select few, and cream of the crop so to speak. This knowledge was not for ordinary Christians. They substituted intellectual knowledge for faith and exalted speculation above the basic tenets, doctrine, and the code of belief. The Apostle John counters with the fact, that there is no private revelation reserved for a few intellectuals, but the entire Body of Believers possesses THE TRUTH of God's Word through faith and not special knowledge.

Chapter 14

LET TRUTH ABIDE IN YOU

Therefore let that abide in you which you heard from the beginning. If what you heard from the beginning abides in you, you will also abide in the Son and in the Father. And this is the promise that He has promised us eternal life. – First John 2:24-25 NKJV

God revealed Himself to us through Jesus Christ, that we might have the light of life within us by the presence of the Holy Spirit. *Our mission* is to let the light abide in us and shine forth to the glory of God. This produces light in the lives of others, and extending fellowship of God. Love for others is the sure sign that God lives in us and that we are in the fellowship of His love.

Jesus is THE TRUTH; He is the original. We've learned of Him from the Gospels and we know the truth from the false. We know Jesus is our Lord and Savior and we know we have everlasting life. We also know that fake people, false preachers, false teachers, and false leaders will come in an attempt to shake us from that truth. However, we have the ability to hear the truth and reject the false. So we don't entertain any thoughts from people who don't know Jesus, and people who promote any other walk of life other than Jesus. We learned of Jesus when He revealed Himself to us and that began our walk with God. Jesus is our new life, our beginning as sons and daughters of God and brothers with Christ. We have taken what we have learned since the beginning of our walk in Christ and have grown in His Word.

When we first heard of Jesus and believed in Him for eternal life, it changed our lives forever. We need to continue to believe in Him, worship Him, and give testimonies about what He has done for us and our family—it's good to brag on God. We need to keep praying with Him and honor Him with our lifestyle. When we do this, the promise of eternal life will be our reality and not just a mere hope.

> These things I have written to you concerning those who try to deceive you. But the anointing which you have received from Him abides in you, and you do not need that anyone teach you; but as the same anointing teaches you concerning all things, and is true, and is not a lie, and just

Let Truth Abide in You

as it has taught you, you will abide in Him.
$$- \text{1 John 2:26-27}$$

The evil art of deception has been practiced for thousands of years. The Nation of Israel has been victimized through deception many times in the past. They had a habit of marrying foreign women and they eventually changed from serving the True and Living God to strange gods because of their lusts of strange women. Instead of being dominant in the ways of Jehovah, they were dominated through the lust of the flesh, (sex), to the point they bowed down and worshipped whatever god their new wives supported.

■ ■ ■

Jesus is THE TRUTH; He is the original. We've learned of Him from the Gospels and we know the truth from the false. We know Jesus is our Lord and Savior and we know we have everlasting life.

An example is in the Book of Numbers. This is one of the most interesting and revealing stories in the Bible. Balak was the King of Moab, a heathen nation that lived in the plains of Moab by the Jordan River and across from Jericho. Balak knew that Israel de-

God's Blueprint

feated Sihon - the king of Amorites, and Og, the king of Bashan and he believed that his nation would be Israel's next victory. Even though God told Israel not to attack Moab, Balak and his people were sick with fear, dread, anxiety, and trepidation on what might happen. They didn't believe God, but they were scared of Him. So Balak sought the Elders of Midian for counsel on how to defeat Israel. Balak knew that he could not defeat Israel in combat, so he and the council decided to fight Israel on a spiritual level.

Balak sought out a *pagan* prophet who would engage Israel in *spiritual warfare* and cause God to cease from protecting her. The Moabites believed that blessing and cursing could be manipulated by skilled agents and Balaam was the most famous agent during this time. Balaam was a prophet who specialized in animal divination. He would inspect the liver of a ritually slain animal to determine the will of the gods. It was his hope that He could entreat the True and Living God to reverse His blessing on the nation of Israel and curse them.

So Balak sent messengers to Balaam, the son of Beor at Pethor, which is near the River in the land of the sons of his people, to call him saying, "Look! A people have come from Egypt. See they have covered the face of the earth, and are settling next to me! Therefore come at once, curse the people for me, for they are too mighty for me. Perhaps I shall be able to defeat them and drive them out of the land, for I know that he whom you bless is blessed and he whom you curse is cursed. – Numbers 22:5-6

The messengers came to Balaam and made their request and Balaam in turn told them to wait until morning. During the night, the Lord came to Balaam and told him not to go with these men and you shall not curse Israel because they are blessed. So Balaam rose early the next morning and told the men that the Lord refuses to give him permission to go with them, so he sent them back to the king.

This cycle continued two more times, Balak tried to pay Balaam with riches, but Balaam continued to say, "I cannot curse what the Lord has blessed." Balak was angry at Balaam because the plan did not work—no one can curse who the Lord has blessed. So Balaam figured if he can't curse what God has blessed he would try another route. He began to counsel the woman of Moab to mingle with the children of Israel, if they could not be destroyed by might, maybe they could be destroyed through spiritual warfare, or sharing God with other gods. The Bible says in Numbers 25:1 that the people of Israel began to commit harlotry with the women of Moab. This harlotry was not just sexual escapades, but also spiritual disobedience because Israel started making sacrifices to the gods of Moab, and they involved themselves sexually with their daughters of Moab. The men of Israel and the daughters of Moab bowed down to false gods and ate food that was sacrificed to these demonic entities freely. The Lord was angry with Israel and sent a plague in which 24,000 people died.

To be honest, Israel was just mere men trying to follow the Ten Commandments without the anointing of God. The only men God anointed in the Old Testament were Kings, Prophets, and Priests.

The kingdom of darkness uses these same tactics today. If agents of darkness cannot beat you one way, they will try another. False prophets like Balaam are active and they mingle with the churches of God to steal, kill and destroy. Open sex and turning one's back on God has always been the tactics of nearly all false prophets because the lust of the eyes and flesh are *strongholds* in the lives of men and woman. Many decide to disobey God's commandments because they believe His commandments are not fun, and they only stifle the lifestyle of most people. As Balaam turned many away from God, there are many leaders in churches today who indulge in the

Let Truth Abide in You

same activities. There are many young people in the Church who wonder why they should even go to services, because leaders are living ungodly lives. Some Pastors, Ministers, divorce their wives only to remarry some *Jezebel* to satisfy their own lusts. [But they call it love.] Others father many children with the unstable women in the church. Once again, when the head of the church is not right—the whole church suffers.

Deception is still strong in the world today but should not be in the Body of Christ. The Holy Spirit warns us about deceivers as they come and as they go. They will make inroads to those who don't know Jesus and their deception has made a home within them in one way or another, one god or another, through one false prophet or another, and they are fine with it—until Judgment Day.

But Jesus came to change mere men into *the sons of God.* Because we are anointed with the Holy Spirit, we are no longer weak and bound by our flesh, [unless we choose to]. It is impossible for the Holy Spirit to lie about anything; so therefore, we should no longer be tossed about by every *wind of doctrine* that comes down the road. We are not empty vessels without a clue, but men of God full of the Holy Spirit. All Christians have an anointing from God,

151

God's Blueprint

an impartation of the Holy Spirit dwells in us. So we acknowledge the indwelling and travel the path of life God called us to do.

The Holy Spirit glorifies Jesus Christ by declaring Him or making Him known to us when we previously did not know Him. It is the work of the Holy Spirit to shed light on Jesus the Christ, Who is the exact imagine of the invisible God. Christ is the center stage which is the desire of God the Father and God the Holy Spirit. The Apostles received truth from the Holy Spirit when they started their individual ministries, truth about Christ and truth about things to come. Then under the guidance of the Holy Spirit they wrote these truths which are known today as the New Testament.

The ministry of the Holy Spirit did not stop after the first century as some believe, He's still teaching believers today, He is still guiding believers today, and He is still showing us things to come today. He abides in us as we abide in Him and His message is still Jesus the Christ and no other.

There are basically two things that will protect believers from falling into the *seductive* teachings of the *heretics*.

Let Truth Abide in You

1. Constantly *abiding* in the truth concerning Jesus the Christ, which we have received from the Holy Bible (The Gospels) written by the Apostles through the Holy Spirit. They took dictation from the Holy Spirit and were witnesses to the teachings of Jesus.

2. The anointing of the Holy Spirit, whose *illuminating* power will enable us to distinguish truth from error. The reason we receive knowledge under the guidance of the Holy Spirit is to know the truth in a way that human instruction cannot provide. I'm not making an argument against the teaching ministry, I am a Teacher myself, I am placing emphasis that only the Holy Spirit is able to bring revelation to the heart. The Teacher shares with the congregation what the Holy Spirit reveals.

If you love Me, keep My commandments. And I will pray the Father, and He will give you another Helper, that He may abide with you forever – the Spirit of Truth, whom the world cannot receive, because it neither sees Him nor knows Him; but you know Him for He dwells with you and will be in you. I will not leave you orphans; I will come to you. – John 14:15-18

Now, if we truly love Jesus, we will keep His commandments. We will love our Lord and Savior and our brothers and sisters in Christ also. Jesus sent The Holy Spirit a little over two thousand years ago to dwell in the saints of God. He started on *the Day of Pentecost* and has been working through the saints ever since. When Jesus ascended the Holy Spirit descended fifty days later, He promised us He would not leave us orphans without help or guidance, and He didn't.

The Holy Spirit is also called the Helper, and *the Comforter*. As a helper, He is our assistant, our aid, our collaborator or colleague and He helps us in our daily lives. The Holy Spirit is assigned to help believers only, He does not help the people of the world, because they cannot receive Him; due to, they either don't know Christ or have rejected Him. But brothers and sisters in Christ know Him because He is made known to us and dwells in us. Now we have something in common with Jesus because our sinful flesh has been *converted* to a holy nature through the Holy Spirit. Old things have passed away and behold, all things become new. (See: 2 Co 5:17) This is the plan of God for all Believers. He offered us life through Jesus the Christ, Who taught us how to live and how to worship God in Spirit and in Truth. When the ministry of Christ was fulfilled, (His death, burial and resurrection), the ministry of the Holy Spirit began for Believers.

Let Truth Abide in You

I still have many things to say to you, but you cannot bear them now. However, when He, the Spirit of Truth, (the Holy Spirit emphasis mine), has come,; and He will tell you things to come. He will glorify Me, for He will take what is Mine and declare it you. All things that the Father has are Mine. Therefore, I said that He will take of Mine and declare it to you."

– John 16:12-15

■ ■ ■

It is impossible for the Holy Spirit to lie about anything; so therefore, we should no longer be tossed about by every wind of doctrine that comes down the road.

Before Jesus was arrested, tried, whipped, hung and died, He told His disciples He had many things to say, many things to teach, but the disciples were unable to understand them, for they had not been born again yet. He was preparing the eleven for *the shift* from His teaching to the Holy Spirit's teaching which happens to be the same teaching, because they are One.

I want you to notice the blueprint here. Remember, Jesus only said what His Father says and does

155

what His Father does. The Holy Spirit will guide you into all truth; for He will not speak on His own authority, as Jesus did not speak on His own authority but whatever He heard from God. As mentioned before, we should only speak what the Holy Spirit speaks and do what the Holy Spirit guides us to do. So when He moves—we move just like that.

When Jesus ascended from the earth to Heaven, the Holy Spirit descended from Heaven to Earth, (See Acts 2). During His earthly ministry, Jesus was an individual, He possessed a body of skin and hair just like the rest of us, He ate like us, drank like us, walked like us, took showers like us, and He was full of the Spirit of God and wisdom. However, He could only be at one place at a time because of His dirt suit or His fleshly body that contained Him physically so He traveled either by foot or on a donkey. The Holy Spirit dwells in believers wherever believers are. If there are believers in France, the Holy Spirit will dwell in the believers in France. It is the same in Mexico, Russia, the United States, Canada, Africa, South America, and Iceland and so on. The Holy Spirit will dwell wherever believers dwell. So instead of being restricted in one place, the Holy Spirit dwells in believers around the world.

He will glorify Me, for He will take what is Mine

and declare it you. All things that the Father has are Mine. Therefore, I said that He will take of Mine and declare it to you" – John 16:15

The Holy Spirit will glorify, praise, worship, adore, exalt, deify, and *lionize* Jesus. The Holy Spirit glorifies Christ by declaring Him and making Him known. It does not mean He will focus on Jesus and not the Father, for Jesus is the image of the invisible God, (cf. Col. 1:15). There is no division in the Godhead, what God has, Jesus has and the Holy Spirit will declare these things to us, the Body of Jesus Christ, the Church, Believers, His sons and daughter. We are to follow the steps the Holy Spirit provides because His instructions come from the throne of God. If we are truly sons and daughters of God, we need to be sensitive to the moving of the Spirit. So let God's Word live in you so you can live in God.

God's Blueprint

Chapter 15
THE CHILDREN OF GOD

And now, little children, abide in Him that when He appears, we may have confidence and not be ashamed before Him at His coming. If you know that He is righteous, you know that everyone who practices righteousness is born of Him. – First John 2:28-29 NKJV

When we are in a relationship with someone, we spend time with that person. As this relationship moves forward, we find out what they like and don't like. We find out their favorite food, music, sports, transportation, television shows, movies, church, and thoughts on any subject. When we spend time in prayer with God, Jesus and the Holy Spirit, we become acquainted with them. When we meditate on His Word, we are relating with Him, when we read His Word, we are learning of Him, when we follow His Word, we are obedient to Him. When we pray with Him, we are developing a relationship with Him. When we to get still, and block the world from our minds, so we can get close to Him. All these activities are abiding in the

God's Blueprint

Lord and the Lord will abide in us. We must remember that abiding in Christ is not only by faith, it is also by living an obedient life.

For Believers, God is love and there isn't any fear serving an awesome God. Jesus says, *"My sheep knows My voice."* When we are in a *relationship* with anyone, we recognize the voice of that person, when we spend time with Jesus we will recognize His Voice also. When we abide, or live in the Word of God we will have confidence, self-assurance, and enthusiasm in Him when He appears. We will not be ashamed, embarrassed, mortified, or reluctant, when He comes. Remember, if we are ashamed of Him, He will be ashamed of us. But if we know Jesus is righteous, and we are *emulating* or practicing His righteous acts, then we'll know we are born of Him.

Behold what manner of love the Father has bestowed on us, that we should be called children of God! Therefore the world does not know us, because it did not know Him. Beloved, now we are children of God and it has not yet been revealed what we shall be, but we know that when He is revealed, we shall be like Him, for we shall see Him as He is. And everyone who has this hope in Him purifies himself, just as He is pure.
– 1 John 3:1-6

160

The Children of God

It is a great privilege to be a recipient of God's great love. Because He bestowed, imparted, and gave His love to believers, and we have received this great and respectable love, we are called children of God. Because we are children of God, the world, (non believers) does not know us because the world did not recognize Christ when He was here and they still don't recognize Him today. It is a terrible thing to be in the world and unable to recognize Christ, the Creator of all things. They didn't recognize Him when He was clothed as a man and they don't recognize Him today. To the world, it's like drowning in the pool and Jesus extends His hands to save you but you don't reach for His hand because you don't know Him. It's like having a million dollars in the bank but you refuse the money and eat out of the garbage can. Jesus came to help us all but a lot of people don't want His help. How stupid is that?

Jesus revealed Himself to men and women who would eventually become sons and daughters of God. Even though He called us before time began, we still had to go through life as heathens before we came to the realization that we needed a Savior. We needed to live a clean and holy life for God.

God has blessed His children. We are now *joint heirs* with Christ because we were redeemed by *the*

God's Blueprint

blood of the Lamb personally. We were chosen before the world was ever created to be blessed by the Lord personally. We are blessed to be the head and not the tail; we are blessed to live above and not beneath. We have personally been forgiven of our sins. We were chosen and blessed to be holy and without blame before Him and in Him. We are a chosen generation, a royal priesthood, a holy nation and special people. We have been chosen by God to be His home, to be the temple of the Holy Spirit upon this earth. We have been chosen by God and Jesus and He is not only our Lord and Savior but He is also our Big Brother. God has bestowed, given, and granted His love upon us, who were at one time not His, but now—we are His children. Even though it has not been revealed what we shall be, we know when Christ is revealed we shall be like Him because we will see Him up close and personal.

Jesus was in the world, and the world was made through Him, and the world did not know Him. He came to His own, and his own did not receive Him. But as many as received Him, to them He gave the right to be children of God, to those who believe in His name: who were born, not of the blood, nor of the will of the flesh, nor of the will of man, but of God. – John 1:10-13

The Children of God

Jesus caused all of us to exist, yet when He came, the world did not know Him? This is like going to visit your children, but your children would not receive you as their parents and to top it all off, even reject you as their parents. Jesus came to Earth, to the people He called into existence ...and they did not receive Him and even refused Him. Believe it or not there are millions of people from all races, tribes, nations and tongues who still refuse Him today. But to believers, He gave us the *legal right* to become the children of God. This is a legal right and a lawful right; and it is officially permitted and authorized by God Himself because we believe Jesus and receive Him as our Lord and Savior.

■ ■ ■

It is a great privilege to be a recipient of God's great love. Because He bestowed, imparted, and gave His love to believers, and we have received this great and respectable love, we are called children of God.

We all (that's you and I), were initially born of the flesh, meaning your parents came together and produced a child; this is born of the flesh. We need to understand that no flesh will make it into the Kingdom of God, because the flesh is evil. We must be

God's Blueprint

born of God to make it into His Kingdom of Heaven and in order to be born of God we must repent of our sins and believe in Jesus as the Christ, the Son of God.

> Beloved, now we are children of God and it has not yet been revealed what we shall be, but we know that when He is revealed, we shall be like Him, for we shall see Him as He is. And everyone who has this hope in Him purifies himself, just as He is pure. – 1 John 3:2

God has not revealed everything to us, and God has not revealed what we shall be. A day is coming when Jesus will be fully revealed; and we shall be like Him because we will see Him as He is. Until then, we who believe this will keep ourselves pure, (separated from the world) just as Jesus is pure.

Chapter 16

SIN AND THE CHILD OF GOD

Whoever commits sin also commits
lawlessness, and sin is lawlessness.
And you know that He was manifest-
ed to take away our sins, and in Him there is no
sin. Whoever abides in Him does not sin. Whoever sins has neither seen Him nor known Him.
– First John 3:4-6 NKJV

Whoever is still sinning is committing lawlessness,
anarchy, chaos, disorder, and mayhem. Point Blank!
Whoever is still sinning does not have control over
anything, including himself. Jesus came into the
world to take away our sins, to cleanse us from all unrighteousness. There was and is no sin in Christ Jesus.
Since we have received the privilege of being a son or
daughter of God, we have the benefit of abiding in
Christ which is living a sinless life from that point on.
This is contrary to most churches' doctrine and beliefs, but the Bible makes it plain; whoever abides in
Christ—does not sin. Whoever does not believe this,
does not know Jesus from a spiritual standpoint, they

God's Blueprint

just know of Him as a historical figure.

This is what I call practicing a mirrored Christianity where people want to go to Heaven without following the doctrine of Christ. I've heard Pastors declare we are Christians, but we still sin. I heard and saw an old lady in the Church smile and say, 'Oh yes, we still sin'. It breaks my heart to hear such confessions because it does not line up with the Word of God. These folks profess to be Christian, but they do not have Jesus even though they've gone to church all their lives.

Why is this? Pastors and Teachers just don't teach the full council of God. They want a happy congregation and happy congregations pay their tithes, give offerings and will work in their church. There is generally a *sugarcoated* sermon where the goodness of Christ is preached, but nothing about the covenant and nothing about God's moral character. These subjects are good, but Pastors don't want to lose their congregation with the hard subjects that are needed for actual Christian living, character and conduct. I believe most haven't received a revelation for righteous living, or rejected the revelation they've witnessed in an attempt to keep what they've got. But the bottom line is: Teachers and Preachers will be judged on what they didn't preach and teach, and they will receive a harsh penalty for their weak-

Sin and the Child of God

ness or *unwillingness* to preach and teach the whole council of God. God did not give us a spirit of fear but of power and of love and a sound mind.

> Little children, let no one deceive you. He who practices righteousness is righteous, just as He is righteous. He who sins is of the devil, for the devil has sinned from the beginning. For this purpose the Son of God was manifested, that He might destroy the works of the devil. Whoever has been born of God does not sin, for His seed remains in him; and he cannot sin, because he has been born of God. – 1 John 3:3-9

The devil has a personal doctrine, an evil doctrine in which living in the flesh is the highest priority. He speaks to carnal men and women to appeal to their feelings, their emotions, their sentiment and their passions. Carnal men and women live exclusively on what they see and take joy in tasting, touching and feeling. "If it feels good, do it!" is their confession. Some say what used to be bad behavior is now accepted as good behavior and vice versa. Deceivers don't know they are deceived and will be vehement, passionate and sometimes violent in justifying their bad or unrighteous behavior.

Jesus came to us and told us we're living in sin. He

told us we won't be able to go to Heaven as sinners because no flesh will enter the Kingdom of God. He told us we need to change our lives and put away our sins, but we couldn't do it. We needed a Savior in Jesus Christ and He did not disappoint. He taught us the right way to live, He taught us how to live holy and righteously. When people believe in the teachings of Jesus, *the works of the devil* are destroyed in their lives. When we repent of our sins and confess Christ Jesus as Lord then we become born again or born of God, and whoever is born of God will not live a sinful life.

■ ■ ■

Jesus came into the world to take away our sins, to cleanse us from all unrighteousness. There was and is no sin in Christ Jesus.

He who practices righteousness, virtue, decency and honesty is righteous as Jesus is righteous. We live our Christian lives by practicing righteous living through God's love, moral conversation, and blameless in our relationship with other people, then we are righteous. Jesus lived righteously in His walk, in His conversation and in His relationships with others. So when we walk as Jesus walked we will be considered righteous just like Jesus.

Sin and the Child of God

He who sins is of the devil, for the devil has sinned from the beginning. — 1 John 3:8a

Think about the following:
If you are still rejecting Christ,
...if you are still stealing,
...if you are still gossiping,
...if you are still lying,
...if you are still getting high,
...if you are still killing and murdering,
...if you are still sexually immoral,
...if you are having sex with minors,
...if you are having same-sex activities,
...if you are sampling flesh every night or on occasion,
...if you are still hating,
...if you are still a racist,
...if you are still dabbling in sorcery,
...if you are still having sex with someone's wife/husband or with whosoever,
...if you are still exhibiting burst of wrath,
...if you are still caught up in selfish ambition,
...if you are still creating and projecting heresy, deviation, dissent, sacrilege,
...if you are still living in drunkenness,
...if you are still participating in revelries,
...if you are still practicing idolatry,
...if you are still practicing lewdness, or any other

unrighteous act,
...then you are of the devil—point blank!

For this purpose the Son of God was manifested, that He might destroy the works of the devil. Whoever has been born of God does not sin, for His seed remains in him; and he cannot sin, because he has been born of God. – 1 John 3:8b-9

Jesus didn't give up His Throne in Heaven and come into this world to party, get high, have sex, and practice unrighteousness on the earth. He didn't come down from Heaven to compromise the Word of God. He didn't come down to just to fit in with the crowd or His peers. He came to save us from our sins, because our sins were killing us and we're laughing, partying and sinning all the way to Hell. He came down to *destroy* the works of the devil. He didn't come down to change the works of the devil, or modify it, or amend it—He came down to destroy the devil's works, to obliterate them, to demolish and completely annihilate his influence, authority, and manipulative actions against man.

Jesus did not save us to continue in sin, He saved us to be free from sin filled activities by changing our nature from a *nature* of sin to a nature of righteousness. It's called, "Born Again," this time it is not

Sin and the Child of God

of flesh, (your parents coming together to create a baby), your nature was changed by God Himself. He spoke to your evil nature and it was destroyed then He imparted His Spirit into your spirit which caused you to be a new and different person, to be *born of God*. God cannot sin and if the spirit of God dwells in you, then you won't sin either.

It is written, 'Man shall not live by bread alone, but by every word that proceeds from the mouth of God. – Matthew 4:4

Now whoever has been born of God does not sin. This is the same God that wrote, prompted, initiated, and activated all the Holy Scriptures. This is about as point blank as can be, yet I haven't heard it preached or taught but a few times. We should believe every Word that proceeds from the mouth of God. This Scripture has been highlighted with black sharpies by people who can't or don't want to know the truth. Or choose to ignore this truth. Or feel it's beyond their ability to live a sin free life. There are many Christians who simply believe they cannot live a life without sin. This sort of thinking is simply unbelief, my friend Gary calls it 'stinking thinking'. Those who feel this way are still under the works of the devil because they do not believe God.

God's Blueprint

John's teaching through the Holy Spirit continues,

Whoever has been born of God does not sin,
for His seed remains in him; and he cannot sin,
because he has been born of God. — 1 John 3:9

■ ■ ■

**God cannot sin and if the spirit of God
dwells in you, then you won't sin either.**

This is probably the most looked-over verse in the
entire Bible. They may quote, "an eye for an eye,"
but refuse to believe we're born of God. We, as children of God should believe this verse, but many do
not. Whoever is born of God does not sin, period,
because the seed of God remains in us. He abides in
us as we abide in the Trinity. Jesus says, *"He came to
cleanse us from all our sins."*

The seed that remains is God's *divine nature* which
has taken residence in our spirit. This is what makes
us different. This is how we can walk the walk of
Christ Jesus.

Chapter 17
THE IMPERATIVE OF LOVE

I n this the children of God and the children of the devil are manifest: Whoever does not practice righteousness is not of God. Nor is he who does not love his brother. For this is the message that you heard from the beginning, that we should love one another, not as Cain who was of the wicked one and murdered his brother. And why did he murder him? Because his works were evil and his brother's righteous.

– First John 3:10-12 NKJV

Through all of this, the children of God and the children of the devil are made known by their deeds or actions. Both of these groups of people, the children of God and the children of the devil have been exposed and uncovered by their works or by their deeds. The children of God are living righteously in our works, deeds, worshipping our God and loving our neighbors. Loving one another is an absolute requirement and necessity in living for Christ and advancing His Kingdom. Righteous living by the fruit of the Spirit and allowing the Holy Spirit to guide, teach, and reveal future events is a must. It is the Christian man and woman's duty, responsibility, and obligation to be obedient to the *instructions* of God by walking by faith and not by sight. These practices of righteousness are of God.

Cain is identified spiritually as a child of the devil. His brother Abel is identified as a child of God. Cain's act of murder was the epitome of hatred back then and still today. Nothing has changed since the first murder, in fact it has gotten worst. In 2016, an average of 43 people were murdered every day. The bottom line is, murder and every other sin is of the devil. So *the children of the devil are manifest* also; every day people of all ages are publically announcing who they serve by their actions. Snipers, school and church shootings, family killings, school and church leaders molesting children, open gay marriages, practicing a homosexual lifestyle, thieving pastors and deacons, racists of all nationalities are practicing discrimination, prejudice, bigotry, and intolerance. These are unrighteous acts. Then there are government officials operating in greed, pride, power, and prestige through the lust of the flesh daily. There's not enough ink and paper to describe all the manifestations of the devil, but we can call it sin. The practices of the people in this paragraph are not of God.

The Imperative of Love

Do not marvel, my brethren, if the world hates you. We know that we passed from death to life, because we love the brethren. He who does not love his brother abides in death. Whoever hates his brother is a murderer, and you know that no murderer has eternal life abiding in him.

– 1 John 3:13-15

My brothers and sisters in Christ, don't be surprised when the world, the people who don't know Jesus, hate us. They will hate us simply because we belong to Christ. They hate us because we have something the world doesn't have—*eternal life*. Since we have this gift of life, they will hate us because we don't live by the world's standards, principles or values. We live by the principles and commandments of God. So don't get upset when we are excluded from worldly events, don't be surprised when they speak of us with venom in their voices. Don't be surprised when they talk about you, curse you, and display irritation and annoyance toward you simply because you belong to Christ. Whoever hates his brother is a murderer and there will not be a single unrepented murderer that will gain eternal life. There will ex-murderers that will obtain eternal life because they repented of their sins and Jesus forgave them.

God's Blueprint

■ ■ ■

Loving one another is an absolute requirement and necessity in living for Christ and advancing His Kingdom.

Love for our brothers and sisters are the *evidence* of being born again; it is the evidence that we have passed from the empire of death to the Kingdom of life. Notice the language here, 'have passed.' This is not an event that will happen in the future; it has already happen and has become a reality in our lives. When we as Christians experience Christ's gift of salvation, we now have the ability to *demonstrate* God's love for our fellow believers right now. We have the ability through Christ's gift of salvation to continue to bear evidence of a changed life. We have the evidence to bear agape right now.

Chapter 18

THE OUTWORKING OF LOVE

By this we know love, because He laid down His life for us. And we also ought to lay down our lives for the brethren. But whoever has the world's goods, and sees his brother in need, and shuts up his heart from him, how does the love of God abide in him? – First John 3:16-17 NKJV

It is almost unfathomable for some people to believe Jesus came to die for our sins and make a way for our salvation. Even though Jesus did this for us, people still hate Him for what He did. And people will hate Christians now for what we do. Jesus laid down His life for us, so we must also lay down our lives for our brothers and sisters in Christ. We must remember that our *true rewards* are not of this earth, because the earth is just a training ground for life in Heaven.

Believers should not be so hung up on the world's goods to the point of selfishness. We need to know that love denies self-interest and our love for our brothers and sisters in Christ should be expressed practically or

God's Blueprint

sensibly. When we see a hungry brother or sister, we should feed Him or her. When we see a thirsty brother or sister, we should give them drink. If we see a brother or sister in need of clothing, then we should clothe them. Jesus said this in Matthew 25:35-40.

For I was hungry and you gave Me food; I was thirsty and you gave Me drink; I was a stranger and you took Me in. I was naked and you clothed Me; I was in prison and you came to Me. Then the righteous will answer Him, saying, "Lord, when did we see You hungry and feed you, or thirsty and gave You drink? When did we see You a stranger and take You in. or naked and clothed You? Or when did we see You sick and come to You." And Jesus answered, "Assuredly I say to you, inasmuch as you did it to the least of these My brother, you did it to Me.

This is Kingdom business here, when we see those in need, we help them. But when we see our brother or sister in need and we don't help, then the love of God doesn't abide in us. NEWSFLASH!!! The people we help do not necessarily have to be Christians. We should help non-believers in their time of need. We can feed them in their time of need, clothe them in their time of need, and give them money in their time of need. When we do these things, we are actually

The Outworking of Love

introducing them to the ways of Christ. This action may entice them to say, "What must I do to be saved?"

Jesus preached a sermon one day and none of them were Christians, but He fed them. In fact some of the people He fed, participated later in His crucifixion. So we need to have the same attitude, the same mind-set, because when you bless someone with any form of kindness you are *showing* the love of Jesus.

> My little children let us not love in word or tongue, but in deed and in truth. And by this we know that we are of the truth and shall assure our hearts before Him. For if our hearts condemns us, God is greater than our heart, and knows all things. Beloved, if our heart does not condemn us, we have confidence toward God. And whatever we ask we receive from Him, because we keep His commandments and do these things that are pleasing in His sight. And this commandment: that we should believe on the name of His Son Jesus Christ and love one another, as He gave us commandment.
>
> – 1 John 3:18-23

Christians should be the most transparent and truthful people on the planet. Therefore our love for one another should be authentic, genuine, reliable, and valid. We should not be involved with lip service on any level, because lip service is a form of lying, we would be wrong if we are not truthful in our words and in our actions. If I say that I'm going to do something and then don't do it, then I'm not much of a Christian. But when I consistently do what I say I'll do and my heart doesn't condemn me, then I'll be pleasing in His sight. I'm not necessarily doing this strictly for my brothers and sisters in Christ—I'm doing this for *God's service*. When we do good deeds for men, we are actually doing them for the Lord. Remember Matthew 25?

■ ■ ■

This is Kingdom business here, when we see those in need, we help them.

By our actions we know that we are of the truth and shall assure, promise, pledge, and declare our hearts before Him. We can be assured of His presence and eternal life within us when we demonstrate self-sacrificial love to others and for others. We know our behavior's source in truth is Christ, so then we know we will have confidence before God. The bottom line is the truth and love of God benefits both the giver of love and the receiver of love. Both parties would be blessed.

The Outworking of Love

If we are playing with the Gospel and not living up to the truth of God's Word, then our hearts will condemn us. When we offer lip service or running our mouths instead of declaring the truth, we'll eventually recognize we didn't measure up to God's standard of love. Then we will become insecure and not have confidence when we stand before God. It's the same as not preaching or teaching the truth of God's Word, at the end of the day our conscience should condemn us. When our conscience condemns us, we should lie out before Him and repent of this sin, ask Him to touch our hearts and renew us, refurbish us, restore us and replenish us back into the truth of His Word.

Our conscience may not acknowledge the loving deeds we have done in the power of the Holy Spirit, but God does, and He is superior to our hearts. We may feel that an encouraging word or a prayer or even a smile or some pocket change for someone is not noticed by God, but we need to know He sees all we do and the reason for why we do it. God takes everything into account including the Lord's atoning work for us at the cross, our yielding to the Holy Spirit for holy use in the Kingdom of God. We need to understand that God is more compassionate toward us than we sometimes are for ourselves.

God's Blueprint

Chapter 19

THE SPIRIT OF TRUTH AND THE SPIRIT OF ERROR

Now he who keeps His commandments abides in Him, and He in him. And by this we know that He abides in us, by the Spirit whom He has given us.
— First John 3:24 NKJV

When we keep His commandments we will abide in Him, live in Him, cohabitate with Him and exist in Him and we know He abides in us, lives in us, cohabitate in us and exist in us, and when this becomes a spiritual reality to us then we are a blessing to all. When we abide in Christ we have a mutual indwelling with Jesus. It's like living in a house with Jesus, but the only difference is you are the house and Jesus is dwelling in your house as you are dwelling in His house.

Do you not know that you are the temple of God and that the Spirit of God dwells in you.
— 1 Corinthians 3:16

This may seem hard to swallow, but it's still a fact. The

God's Blueprint

Word of God is eternally true. If you're a born again believer, then the Spirit of God dwells in you. Some people skip these verses about God dwelling in them because they believe it is farfetched, fabricated made up idea. Then there are some who don't want God in their business; while, others simply do not believe they could be God's temple because of their involvement in hidden activities. When we lock into these lines of thinking, we're injuring ourselves spiritually because we do not believe what God says. When we don't believe what God says, we are actually calling Him a liar. You will see on Judgment Day that God wasn't lying on any subject, but it will be too late because you've made your bed in the lake of fire, burning day and night forever. Your worldly wishes and prayers will burn up with you when the smell of brimstone becomes a dreadful reality. Stinking thinking will destroy all who do not believe God, or attempt to change His Word, or voting against Christ's commands or simply rejecting Him. But the fact is, God dwells in all of His believers who keep His commandments. It is as simple as that!

> For I know the thoughts that I think toward you, says the Lord, thoughts of peace and not of evil, to give you a good future and a hope.
> – Jeremiah 29:12

God did not create us to punish us or to use us as a

whipping board. God is not cruel; He is a peaceful God, a loving God, a faithful God and a forgiving God. His plans for us are thoughts of peace and not pandemonium, chaos, nor evil. God desires to give us a good future and a hope. God's plan is for us is to live in the light and not the darkness.

- God has already blessed believers with every spiritual blessing in Christ Jesus. He did not say He's going to do it—He's already done it.

- We were chosen to be in Christ before the foundation of the planet.

- We were chosen to be holy and without blame before Him in love.

- He predestined us to be adopted as His sons and daughters through Jesus Christ.

- He redeemed us from the curse of the law.

- We were redeemed through His blood, for the forgiveness of our sins.

- He gave us talents and gifts through His Spirit for us to bless others and to live a truly successful Godly life.

- The Spirit of God dwells in us and we dwell in the Spirit of God

God's Blueprint

There are many other benefits He gave us that we don't even know about, but we will, if we keep His commandments by loving Him and living our lives as true believers day in and day out, He will continue to keep His blessings in and on our lives. We will have troubles and circumstances, situations and problems, but God will be with us as He was with Moses, as He was with David, as He was with Gideon, as He was with Joshua, as He was with Paul, as He was with Jesus, as He was with the disciples, and the Apostles and all believers. He will never leave us nor forsake us because He abides in us and we abide in Him.

> Beloved, do not believe every spirit, but test the spirits, whether they are from God; because many false prophets have gone out into the world. By this you know the Spirit of God: Every spirit that confesses that Jesus Christ has come in the flesh is of God, and every spirit that does not confess that Jesus Christ has come in the flesh is not of God. And this is the spirit of the Antichrist which you have heard was coming, and is now already in the world. – 1 John 4:1-3

There's a lot of conversation crossing the airwaves around the world. We are in an age of universal communication and every subject is up for conversation from politics, to immigration, to health care, to abortions, to climate warming, to sports, to car insurance, and transportation in all their forms, groceries, houses, restaurants, tariffs and taxes, to medical services, marijuana use, the latest fashions, and so on. The world speaks and the like-minded citizens of the world listen to what their friends and colleagues have to say.

■ ■ ■

God desires to give us a good future and a hope. God's plan is for us is to live in the light and not the darkness.

There is a constant train of voices around the world and also in the spirit world. We need to be careful of who we listen to, because every spirit is not of God and we have to discern the origin of these spirits that crosses our paths from day to day. There are many false prophets that are out in the world trying to wrangle in all who will listen and join their cause against the True and Living God. It is a given that the world listens to the world or listens to the false prophets' rhetoric.

There are millions of evil spirits roaming the earth seeking those they can devour. These spirits attempt to *influence* men and women around the world to rebel against God in one form or another. These demon spirits promote racism, hatred, greed, sexual immorality, power, a hunger and thirst for world domination, and organizations and companies against God and Christ and all other activities in the flesh. These evil spirits have been roaming the world since or before the Garden of Eden and there are still thousands if not billions in the world today. Even though Jesus created all angels, one third *rebelled* against God, Jesus and the Holy Spirit. It's a wonder Satan and his rebellious demons and devils weren't destroyed with just one Word from the mouth of God. Jesus created the world with Words, so surely He could destroy the devil and his imps with a Word.

God has allowed Satan and his demons to run their course. When the fullness of time comes to a close, they will be handled according to their deeds, just as men will be judged according to their deeds. Until then, devils and demonic spirits roam the earth seeking victims to steal their salvation and joy, or to kill them before they can receive salvation, and destroy all who are influenced by them. *Religion* is one of the devil's greatest subjects for thousands if not millions who have lost their lives to fleshly belief systems.

The devil is the father of evil spirits and God is the Father of all that is good. Mankind's first recorded encounter with an evil spirit was in the garden where

The Spirit of Truth and...

he deceived Eve into eating the forbidden fruit of the Tree of Life. As mentioned before, Eve was not frightened by the sight or the conversation of Satan. When he came to her, she didn't show signs of fear, terror, or panic as she conversed with the devil. This is one case where *ignorance* is not bliss. Satan was talking to her as a concerned friend, a buddy, or a companion. The devil is a prime example of smiling in your face only to deflate our fears and concerns, but is secretly waiting for the moment to destroy you through his evil conversation.

Evil spirits are forever attempting to induce *doubt* in God's Word. The most common phrase is, "Did God really say that?" Or, did God really mean this or *maybe* He really means that. A woman from the Seventh Day Adventist told me that "God didn't really mean unbelievers will stay in Hell forever, but only for a little while." When she told me that, my spirit reared up I never went back to their service again. Then there was a Deacon from an Episcopal church that taught God ordains gay men for leadership in the church. We went back and forth on the issue for a while and he didn't change his stance and I wasn't going to change mine, because I know what God said…. I didn't go back to that service and he died a few months later. Another man tried to convince me it wasn't the fruit of the garden that caused the fall of mankind, he tried to convince me the devil had sex with Eve and this was the true reason for the fall. He was convinced it couldn't have been the fruit but sex with Eve. One man claimed he was the pastor of four or five churches only to find out he wasn't even the Pastor of one, furthermore he taught tongues is of the devil and not of God. I certainly did not go back. A famous preacher (whom I've never met), claimed the devil will be forgiven and will sit on the left hand of God's throne, while Jesus will sit on the right hand of God. Some of these are just personal examples of false prophets changing the Word, because in all actuality, they hate God. So we must discern the spirits that are driving men in their conversations. If their rendition, interpretation, or version does not match God's Word—then they are evil spirits.

Most of the Catholic Church has been out of the will of God for centuries. The devil has been influencing the Pope for years in *demonic creeds* of evil thoughts and actions. The Pope believes he is the only one on the earth that has the ability to talk or even hear from God. He also endorses gay relationships and marriages. Then there are the thousands of acts of pedophilia throughout the years where young boys are raped without any consequences. The Holy Spirit does not partake in theses ideologies, philosophies, dogma, or beliefs, because it is against the will of God.

The Spirit of Truth and...

The Bible warns us not to believe every spirit, but *test* them to see if they are of God. God gave us a failsafe exercise to protect His children from false prophets. The test is to ask the spirit if he can confess that Jesus has come in the flesh. If the spirit can say this, then the spirit is of God. If the spirit cannot confess that Jesus Christ has come in the flesh is not of God.

I have personally put this to the test and have found it to be true. I asked a Muslim if Jesus came down from Heaven in the flesh and he denied it, in fact you must reject Jesus as the Son of God to become a Muslim. I learned this from personal experience. I asked a Wiccan the same thing and he denied it. I asked a guy who had no particular church but he denied it also. These spirits who can't confess that Jesus came down in the flesh are driving these false prophets to deceive entire nations. They are using false prophets to mislead many on the truth of Christ. They are generating new religions, cults, and antichrist groups to come against the Words of Jesus and they are very tricky at it. Just as Eve was deceived with a smile and non-threatening words, spirits will intrigue and fascinate lost people in the same way. Some will be quiet and stealthy in their deception while others will use great swelling words to impress and deceive men and women.

God's Blueprint

Test the spirits and you will find that many do not align with the Gospel of Christ. These are antichrist. But the spirits that are aligned with the Word of God are your brothers and sisters in Christ. It's just that simple.

For such are false apostles, deceitful workers, transforming into apostles of Christ. And no wonder! Satan himself transforms himself into an angel of light. Therefore it is no great thing if his ministers also transform themselves into ministers of righteousness, whose end will be according to their works. – 2 Corinthians 11:14-15

The words of a false prophet will cause a believer's spirit to be troubled because it doesn't line up with the Word of God. But the Holy Spirit within the believer will warn him/her of the origin of the false prophets and his *agenda*. The false prophet and his followers will use the Name of Jesus flippantly, frivolously, dismissively, superficially, and facetiously. They will claim Jesus is not the way of salvation but a good man who did good deeds years ago. They will say He, Jesus, is dead. They will go to great lengths to offer a new way to God through works, money and false humility. Sexual immorality will be a common thread, and the love of money, power, and greed will be displayed in daily life. False prophets will give the people what they want in order to live as they want to live and believe they're still going to Heaven.

They will teach in the pretense of the Gospel of Christ, but the Gospel will be butchered and massacred and this can only send you directly to Hell. Like the Gnostics, Jesus will be *misrepresented* in His teachings and daily living. The moral character of Christ will be diminished into the immoral doctrine of Satan and yet many will defend this foul and devilish doctrine to the death. I've heard some people even say they're an ambassador of God with a new religion, since Christianity didn't work.

> By this you know the Spirit of God: Every spirit that confesses that Jesus Christ has come in the flesh is of God, and every spirit that does not confess that Jesus Christ has come in the flesh is not of God. This is the spirit of the Antichrist.
> – 1 John 4:2-3

As sons and daughters of the King, we must be cautious in our warfare because the devil will present himself as an *angel of light*. The devil will present himself as Jesus in an atmosphere you've never experience. For instance, my cousin had a severe stomach ailment named diverticulitis. During the time of this ailment, he had a vision and thought it was Jesus coming to him to heal him of this ailment, but this spirit turned away and refused to heal him. Now the devil comes to steal, kill and destroy but Jesus came for us to have life. This brother passed away about a month later because he believed the lie. He thought Jesus didn't want to heal him and when you get a thought like that imbedded in your mind, it's over. It was the devil *transformed* into an angel of light on an assignment to end his life and his unique ministry. This brother was in so much pain; he didn't perform the acid test and believed it was Jesus who came to him. We must realize the devil can transform himself in to an angel of light and call himself Jesus, he can also create a false sense of glory that will seem real but it will be as false as his doctrine. This is why God gave us the test.

■ ■ ■

Test the spirits and you will find that many do not align with the Gospel of Christ. These are antichrist. But the spirits that are aligned with the Word of God are your brothers and sisters in Christ. It's just that simple.

As brothers and sisters in this world, we need to recognize the true and the false. If these spirits cannot

The Spirit of Truth and...

say, "Jesus came down in the flesh" then you're in contact with a devil.

> Greater is He that is in you than He that is in the world. – 1 John 4:4

Greater is the Holy Spirit that dwells in us than the devil that *manipulates* the world to do evil. The devil is the prince of the power of the air and is universal, but Jesus is greater than the devil on all levels. And everyone who is born again, a partaker of the Heavenly Father and His Son and has the indwelling of the Holy Spirit is greater than the devil. When we accepted Christ, The Holy Spirit came into our bodies and made us—His Temple. He is there to teach us the ways of God, to confirm the Scriptures in our spirit, to comfort us, and to show believers things to come. He will also throw a red flag to warn His followers in their spirit when they are accosted by evil forces. When I hear statements that run afoul with the Word of God, I'll try to discuss it and try to redirect this person back to the truth. If they receive it the Word of truth then that's fine, but if not I'm out of there.

> Adulterers and adulteresses! Do you not know that friendship with the world is enmity with God? Whoever wants to be a friend of the world makes himself an enemy of God. – James 4:4

God's Blueprint

We cannot serve two masters. We cannot serve Jesus and the devil. We cannot serve money and Jesus. We cannot continue to choose our wealth, houses, cars, sports; or anything, that walks, crawls, flies or is made by the hands of men that pushes our relationship with God to the side. We cannot go to church and praise the Lord on Sundays and live like h-e-l-l through the week. If we live to satisfy our flesh, then we've made ourselves an enemy of God. If we are chasing the newest fad, the newest thing, the newest fashion or cult constantly, then we're living in adultery and have made ourselves an enemy of the Trinity.

World politics, for the most part, have pushed the doctrine of Jesus to the side. World leaders are counseling each other instead of taking counsel from God. The lust of the eyes and the pride of life are active and very strong in world leaders today. Leaders are arguing, slinging mud, practicing sexual immorality and even fist fighting, all while trying to get a piece of the pie. They are *abusing* taxpayer money for lavish vacations and living daily like movie stars. These people do not realize they have made themselves an enemy of God. The wages they are piling up will bring them to a payday they won't want.

Note: It will be leaders with similar character flaws that will outlaw Christianity and then persecute believers because it is against the lifestyle of the world; as a result, many brothers and sisters in Christ will be killed for it. This will not diminish God's power, or His wisdom. When one dies for the Name of Christ, or in service to Christ they will be blessed and they will be in the presence of God the Father and God the Son forever.

> They are of the world. Therefore they speak as of the world, and the world hears them. We are of God. He who knows God hears us, he who is not of God does not hear us. By this we know the spirit of truth and the spirit of error.
> – 1 John 4:5-6

The people who are lost, or (without Jesus), are the people of the world. When the people of the world speak, then like-minded people will hear them, understand them, and most will agree. Like the saying, "Birds of the feather flock together." The people of the world only understand the things of the world, the lust of the flesh, lust of the eyes and the pride of life and are unable to even hear or understand anything about the True and Living God.

On the flipside, God's people hear Him. Jesus said in John 10, His sheep, (born again believers), know His Voice and He calls us by our name. The voice of

God's Blueprint

strangers or the world, we will not follow because the voice is not the Voice of Jesus. By this we know the Spirit of Truth and *the spirit of error*. The spirit of error is the controlling factor of the world. The world will scream it's political and anti-god policies; enact them as law of the land in order to brainwash and conform Christians to believe in their evil or ungodly ideals, but when Disciples of Christ hear it, we identify it and call it what it really is—Satanic.

My brothers and sisters in Christ do not chase the things of this world, because if we do, we make God our enemy, and that my friends, will be devastating.

> You are of God, little children, and have overcome them, because He who is in you is greater than he that is in the world, they are of the world. Therefore they speak as of the world, and the world hears them. We are of God. He who knows God hears us; he who is not of God does not hear us. By this we know the spirit of truth and the spirit of error. – 1 John 4:4-6

It is a privilege to be a believer, and a child of God, we have overcome these evil spirits because the Holy Spirit that lives, dwells or abides in us is greater, more powerful, and wiser than the devil that leads or influences the world. As far as God is concerned, there are only two languages that are spoken; the language of the world and the language of the saints. The language of the world is the language of darkness, defeat, ignorance, and rebellion. The language of believers is filled with faith, love, wisdom, knowledge, compassion and prayers with God. The world does not understand the language of believers so they speak to one another, hear one another, and understand one another. The world hears the world, they do not hear God.

But we are of God and we hear from God, and we talk with God. We converse with God and we listen to what God tells us and others who know God will hear and understand other believers in Christ. The world and believers of Christ Jesus have nothing in common. In John 17:9 Jesus says,

> "I do not pray for the world but for those You have given Me, for they are yours.

When you are evangelizing or sharing the Word of God and they don't understand you, then they are of the world. Now everyone on the planet begins life in the world, but when the Word of God is spoken, and the ministry of Jesus is believed, the person will be transformed from their lost position in the world to a child of the True and Living God. So he who

God's Blueprint

hears us is of God but he who does not hear us is not of God. By this we know the difference of the Spirit of Truth and the spirit of error.

Chapter 20
KNOWING GOD THROUGH LOVE

B eloved, let us love one another, for love is of God; and everyone who loves is born of God and knows God. He who does not love does not know God, for God is love. In this the love of God is manifested toward us, that God has sent His only begotten Son into the world, that we might live through Him.
                                    – First John 4:7-11 NKJV

For the third time the Apostle Paul stresses love as a test of Christian life. If there's no love for your fellow Christian, then there isn't any knowledge of Jesus; and given that, if you don't have Jesus, then you really don't know God. Believers should love one another, because it shares an attribute with God simply—God is love. Since we are sons of God then love should be our main characteristic, our main quality and feature. Also it is proof of our spiritual rebirth, or our born again experience with Christ. Knowing God

God's Blueprint

is not just head assent. Truly knowing God is an intimate, close, and cherished experiential knowledge gained through our relationship with Him. This is *evidence* of our spiritual birth in God.

Everyone who loves their brothers and sisters in Christ is born of God. When we are born again, born anew, or born of God, one of the first blessings we receive is *the love of God* through the nature of God. To be born again is to believe in Christ, be baptized if possible, repent of our sins and ask Jesus to come in our lives. Then God deposits His Spirit of life into those who believe Christ. Without this spiritual rebirth a person cannot perceive, distinguish, or recognize spiritual matters nor enter into the Kingdom of God. There was a point in our lives when we didn't love God but God loved us and showed His great love for us by sending His only begotten Son to die a horrible death that we might be saved and born again in order to gain entrance into Heaven.

Haters do not know God. Racists do not know God. Murderers do not know God. The sexually immoral do not know God. If you love to sin and you practice sin then you don't know God either, for God is love. No love – no God! I'm not talking about loving your spouse, your parents, children, cousins and family members, that's a different type of love. The love

Knowing God Through Love

God wants us to practice is an *unconditional* love. The kind that's full of forgiveness, and transparent called *Agape*, the kind of love that doesn't hate but is gentle, giving and true.

■ ■ ■

Since we are sons of God then love should be our main characteristic, our main quality and feature.

In the Gospel of John 3:3, there's a story about a Pharisee named Nicodemus, he was a ruler of the Jews. Because he held such a high position in the Sanhedrin, he couldn't afford to visit Jesus during the day. But his curiosity got the best of him and he went to see Him at night. He knew Jesus was someone special because He performed miracles and signs the world has never seen. When he got there he called Him *Rabbi* and continued, "We know You are a great teacher from God." He said this because Jesus was a man that did impossible feats and miracles. Jesus said to him,

> "Most assuredly, I say to you, unless one is born again, he cannot see the kingdom of God"
> – John 3:3 NKJV

Nicodemus was confused, much like the world and some churches today. He couldn't see the spiritual side of this statement for it was foreign or unfamiliar to him. The first thing he thought was climbing back into his mother's womb and reemerging. That's worldly thinking instead of spiritual thinking.

> Most assuredly, I say to you, unless one is born of water and the Spirit, he cannot enter the kingdom of God. That which is born of flesh is flesh and that which is born of Spirit is spirit.
> – John 3:5-6

We all are born of water or natural birth. Our mothers and fathers came together and created a baby like you and I. This is born of the flesh. Everyone who is born of the flesh, God calls an 'evil nature. We were sinners at birth but *the plan* of God was to change us from sinners into saints through the born again process. Everyone born of sexual intercourse is flesh, but when we're born of God, we are born by His Spirit.

> Behold, I was brought forth in iniquity, and in sin my mother conceived me. – Psalms 51:5

Brought forth in iniquity can be translated as brought forth from wickedness, evil, or crime. We may have been cute little babies, but we were born with a sin nature. In order for us to enter the Kingdom of God we must be born of God.

Knowing God Through Love

He who does not love does not know God, for God is love. – 1 John 4:8

Those who do not love their brothers and sisters do not know God. They may think they know God but they don't. The affects of this type of stinking thinking will result in a false relationship with God, which will lead to false religions supported with false doctrines through false spiritual believers. I like to call them unbelieving believers.

Leaders who say they love God but don't, (lip service), will lead their congregations without the Holy Spirit. Therefore, the sermons will be without truth and amiss according to the spirit. The choir will only have only a hand full of songs with lyrics of doubt and disbelief and call it praise and worship. No revelation leads to minimum or no spiritual growth. It is a shame to be on the same spiritual level for multiple years due to a lack of love for God. These folks say they're saved but they don't do anything with their salvation.

In this the love of God is manifested toward us, that God has sent His only begotten Son into the world, that we might live through Him.
– 1 John 4:9

In this love, Jesus is the *manifestation* of God on

God's Blueprint

earth. God is manifested or made known to us, His children, and He has blessed us with revelation knowledge of Jesus the Christ, and we know God sent His Son into the world that we might live through Him. God is so serious about His will or plans for His sons and daughters on the earth, He sent God the Holy Spirit to live in us so that we can live through Him. Remember the Great Commission? God's mission is about saving souls by believers sharing Christ with others, so they too may become believers through Him.

When Jesus dwells in us, we have life and life more abundantly because we have the opportunity to live our lives full of the Holy Ghost. Remember, as God worked through Jesus in His earthly ministry, the Holy Spirit is working, directing, and guiding our lives and ministries. We will say what God says and do what God does. This is living through Him.

> In this love, not that we loved God, but that He loved us and sent His Son to be the propitiation for our sins. Beloved, if God so loved us, we also ought to love one another. – 1 John 4:10-11

Before we were born again we didn't have any love for God. In fact, we had some idea of God but didn't know Him personally at all. A lot of people thought

Knowing God Through Love

of God as sitting on the throne with a big stick to smack us every time we cussed or had sex outside of marriage, or murdered someone, or stole something. That's not God's character, nor His intention for His children. But while we were still sinners God sent His only begotten Son into the world to die for our sins two thousand years ago, He became our *propitiation*, our substitute to appease the wrath of God for all the offenses, all of our iniquities, all of our crimes, all of our sins, all of our transgressions, and all of our waywardness we committed in our formal sinful lives. The *wages of sin* is death and we were working on our wages in the crimes we committed against God and our fellow man. It should have been us (mankind), going to the cross to die for our wild and reckless living. But God sent Jesus to die for our sins and to cleanse us from all unrighteousness. God did this because He loves us. He knew we would have troubled lives and He prepared a way for us to receive eternal life through His only begotten Son, Jesus the Messiah—Jesus the Christ. Since God loves us so much that He sent His Son to die for us, we should be in love with God and love one another.

God's Blueprint

Chapter 21
SEEING GOD THROUGH LOVE

No one has seen God at any time. If we love one another, God abides in us, and His love has been perfected in us. By this we know we abide in Him, and He in us, because He has given us of His Spirit. And we have seen and testify that the Father has sent His Son as Savior of the world. Whoever confesses that Jesus is the Son of God, God abides in him, and he in God. And we have known and believed the love that God has for us. God is love and he who abides in love abides in God and God in Him.

– First John 4:12-16 NKJV

No one has seen God at any time. Now Moses saw God's back from the cleft in the rock when He passed by, but he was not allowed to see God's face. If we love one another then God dwells, resides, inhabits, and lives in us by His Spirit. Because He has given us His Spirit, *we know* He abides in us. God doesn't flippantly give His Spirit to anyone, He can but He doesn't. He gives His Spirit to those who love Him and who love one another. The Apostle John was an eye witness to all of the accounts of Jesus and he declares He has seen and testifies that God sent His only begotten Son into the world to seek and save all that's lost. This is TRUTH! When we confess Jesus as the Son of God, then God abides, dwells, resides, and lives in us by His Spirit and we dwell, reside, and live in Him by our spirit.

■ ■ ■

We were sinners at birth but the plan of God was to change us from sinners into saints through the born again process.

All of this comes down to if we do or if we don't. If we love one another, then God *abides* in us. Point blank! If we love one another He has been *perfected* in us. Remember love is kind and does not envy. Love is not greedy or self-centered. Love does not parade itself or make a spectacle of itself; love doesn't display itself or show off. Love is not puffed up nor does it behave proudly, or swollen, or inflated or inflamed. Love does not behave rudely and is not selfish. Love does not provoke, incite, aggravate, hassle, or irritate others. Love doesn't think evil thoughts and certainly disdains evil deeds. Love doesn't rejoice in iniquity, wickedness, evil, sin, crime, or injustice.

Seeing God Through Love

There are basically four types of love and the most common is *Eros*, which is a physical sexual desire and not much else. This is not the kind of love God is wants from His children to share with others. *Philos* is another Greek word for love and it is based on esteem and affection found in casual friendship. We refer this as brotherly love. *Storge* is a Greek word for family love. *Agape* is the love God wants us to practice; it is based on a deliberate choice of the one who loves rather than the worthiness of the one who is loved. This type of love goes against human nature. It is a giving love, a selfless love and expects nothing in return. It is an unconditional, unrestricted, unreserved, and absolute love. It is a *pure* love that is true and perfect. Love rejoices in THE TRUTH, and it bears all things, believes all things, hopes all things and endures all things. Love never fails. God expects believers to live life in agape.

By this we know we abide in Him, and He in us, because He has given us of His Spirit. And we have seen and testify that the Father has sent His Son as Savior of the world. Whoever confesses that Jesus is the Son of God, God abides in him, and he in God. And we have known and believed the love that God has for us. God is love and he who abides in love abides in God and God in Him. – 1 John 4:13-16

God's Blueprint

You know, this may seem redundant but it's important. Jesus has a habit of repeating Himself, because He wants us to know, register, or identify whatever it is He is teaching. Sometimes we may have to hear something or see something several times before we can come to an understanding about that particular spiritual matter. The Apostle John through the Holy Spirit must believe it's important for us to know that we abide in Christ and Christ abides in us. Think of how powerful the above Scripture reads. The Creator of all there is abides in us, lives in us, by His Spirit. As God's children we have something the world doesn't have or even understand. The Creator lives in us like we live in our homes and we live in His home. Whoever confesses that Jesus is the Son of God, God abides in or lives in Him, and He abides in God. This is stronger than any compact, marriage, or contract in all of creation.

Chapter 22
THE CONSUMMATION OF LOVE

L ove has been perfected among us in this: that we may have boldness in the Day of Judgment; because as He is, so are we in this world. There is no fear in love; but perfect love cast out fear, because fear involves torment. But he who fears has not been made perfect in love. We love Him because He first loved us.
— First John 4:17-19 NKJV

Perfected love in the believers has been *manifested* to rule in our hearts. God has destroyed the fear in our hearts and as we begin a new life with love being our strong suit, love will be perfected in us. We received the *ability* to love from the Father and we cultivate our acts of kindness, acts of compassion, and benevolence with humanity. Like building your money in a savings account, the more love we deposit into others, the greater our love account will be.

Love perfects us, because we know and practice the

truth of God's Word. We don't have the spirit of fear but of love, power, and a sound mind. There is an absence of fear in our hearts because we have been in a relationship with the Trinity. We have been abiding, living and dwelling in God the Father, God the Son and God the Holy Spirit so it is impossible to have any fear in our lives. Because of this, as Jesus is, so are we in the world. As Jesus lives, we will live as the Holy Spirit guides us in our lives. Jesus has a tremendous love for the world to the point that He was beaten several times, a crown of thorns was thrust upon His head, He was mocked, ridiculed, laughed at and scorned before He went to the cross to die for our sins. Then He prayed for those who treated Him terribly, dreadfully, horribly and appallingly by saying, *"Forgive them for they know not what they do!"*

Possessing God's love results in *fearless* confidence toward God and love for the brothers and sisters in Christ. For the believers who know this love have no dread, no fear, no trepidation or anxiety of facing God on Judgment Day.

We can tell who lives in fear and who doesn't. The ones who live in fear, their conversations are, "I hope someone doesn't break in my house, or I need my pistol in case someone tries to rob me, I hope I don't get shot or have a car accident, or I hope my

The Consumation of Love

house don't burn up, or I hope I don't get cancer, and so on and so on." Perfect love cast out fear. If we know God and we're living as we know God, then there's nothing to fear.

One of the benefits, or gifts, or talents of being a believer is that we will have boldness on the Day of Judgment. We know that we know that we know. We know we are born again, we know we are no longer sinners, we know we are no longer haters, we know that the love of God abides in us; we know that we have passed from death to life because we are obedient to His will and His Word. A perfected love produces confidence as we anticipate Jesus' judgment on the world. So our love for God, Jesus, the Holy Spirit, our brothers and sisters in Christ will cause us not to be ashamed when Jesus returns for His Church.

■ ■ ■

Whoever confesses that Jesus is the Son of God, God abides in or lives in Him, and He abides in God. This is stronger than any compact, marriage, or contract in all of creation.

There is *no fear* in love and perfect love cast out fear, because fear involves torment. The world will be in fear on *Judgment Day* because they rejected Christ for some reason or another or misrepresented Him and the Word He brought to us. They rejected love. The world certainly falls short of loving one another and because of this, they are tormented now and will be tormented with the unknown before they are sentenced to their final destination. He who fears has not been made perfect in love.

Chapter 23
OBEDIENCE BY FAITH

I f anyone says, "I love God," and hates his brother, he is a liar; for he who does not love his brother whom he has seen, how can he love God whom he has not seen? And this commandment we have from Him: that he who loves God must love his brother also.
                                        – First John 4:20-21 NKJV

There are a lot of people who say they love God. But the fact is they really don't know Him. Jesus calls this, "lip service." People can say all the right things but it is their hearts that gives them away. There are millions, if not billions of people on this earth who claim to love God, but hate people of other races, they hate people with a different social status, they hate people really just to hate. A heart of hatred is hard to hide for very long and it is eventually exposed. And of course, you can't hide anything from God. A good example is the Catholic Church; the leaders of this organization claim to love God, but do not allow the correction of their priests who sexually violate young

God's Blueprint

boys in their church. When a claim of pedophilia is reported, the leaders just sweep it under the rug and just move the offenders to another cathedral without correction, alteration, or even a rebuke; thus further opportunities to rape and molest more boys is sure to come. There's no *accountability* there. They say they love God, but they have raped children. Sexual crimes such as these are a form of hatred.

It is not just the Catholic Church, there are many, many churches who say they love God but are disobedient and commit crimes toward His Word or keep Him on the back burner. Some have let pride and greed come between them and the Father. When we claim to love God but our actions contradict our lip service, we're liars and don't love Him, or the ones that are made in His image, then we'll have problems.

But the Church, the Body of believers must be a tight group of like-minded people. Our thoughts should align with the thoughts and teachings of Jesus and should be a top priority in our lives. We haven't seen God yet, but we love Him and our brothers and sisters in sincerity and genuineness. As believers, we must *demonstrate* the evidence of love for God for our brothers and sisters in Christ on our daily basis. If we say we love God, but we hate our brother or sister then we're not believers but hypocrites, and

218

Obedience by Faith

liars. So if a believer hates his brother and sister whom he sees daily, how can he love God whom he hasn't seen? We must treat people right because our salvation depends on it. For if we don't treat people right, and then we disqualify ourselves from eternal life and sign up for eternal damnation. This is a commandment from Jesus, he who loves God, must love his brother and sister also.

Jesus taught *a parable* about a man traveling from Jerusalem to Jericho. Along the way he was robbed, stripped of his clothing, wounded, and severely beaten. By chance, a priest came by and saw him but he passed him by. Also a Levite saw the naked and beaten man and he also passed him by. But a Samaritan came by and saw the victim whose been beaten down, stripped of his clothes and left for dead had a different spirit, a godly spirit. Unlike the priest and Levite, the Samaritan had *compassion* for the victim. He bandaged his wounds and poured wine and oil on them. Then he set the wounded man on his own animal and took him to the Inn, a place of recovery. The next day he took two denarii and gave them to the Inn Keeper and told him to take care of him and if he spends more than this, he promised to repay whatever was spent. While the Priest and Levite didn't bother with the wounded man the Samaritan show extraordinary compassion on the crime victim. Now the priest and the Levite have both

God's Blueprint

claimed their love for God, but their actions proved them to be liars.

Both the Priest and the Levite were in covenant with God. They were ordained to take care of the spiritual needs of God's people, to counsel them by the Word of God, to encourage them by the Word of God, to pray for them and to meet their needs, both spiritual and physical, according to the Word of God. However, both these men went around the wounded man and did not meet his needs, but left him for dead. This action dictates the lack of love for God, they wore the apparel of knowing God, but their hearts revealed who and what they were. The compassion of God was nowhere to be found in these men. I believe this Samaritan, a half Jewish person, loved God and his love for God was demonstrated by his actions to care for the fallen person. This Samaritan acted more like a believer than the Priest and the Levite who were called by God into these positions.

Whoever believes that Jesus is the Christ is born of God, and everyone who loves Him who begot also loves him who is begotten of Him. By this we know that we love the children of God, when we love and keep His commandments.
— 1 John 5:1-2

Obedience by Faith

Whoever believes that Jesus is the Christ, the Anointed One is born of God, or *born again*. Because God chose us to be born of the Spirit, we are truly sons and daughters of God. The condition of being born of God is to believe, trust and accept as truth, the life and Gospel of Jesus the Christ. This spiritual rebirth is reflected in the love of our brothers and sisters who have been born into the family of God. The reason why the subject of love is stressed upon us, is that it is important that we get this. The Holy Spirit sees how we react in situations every day. The thing is, do we respond in love, or indifference. So let us continue to respond in the love of Christ by the Word of Christ.

> For this is the love of God, that we keep His commandments. And His commandments are not burdensome. For whatever is born of God overcomes the world. And this is the victory that has overcome the world – our faith. Who is he who overcomes the world, but he who believes that Jesus is the Son of God? – 1 John 5:3-5

Believers believe. What people believe, and who they believe in makes a big difference in their quality of life on Earth and their destination after death. Whoever believes Jesus is the Christ is born of God or *regenerated* by God, having passed from death to life and will spend eternal life with the Trinity. Everyone

221

who loves God is begotten, or born of God and also loves all the children of God. Loving and keeping His commandants proves we are children of God.

The love of God demands *obedience*. Some find it difficult to be obedient to God and His command. However, God's commands are not burdensome, taxing, or arduous, because His Spirit dwells in you and your new nature, your changed life makes your God experience a reality. God commands every believers to be the people we were created to be: holy beings that clearly mirror the image of God. True Believers practice what is real, because the True and Living God is real.

■ ■ ■

This is a commandment from Jesus, he who loves God, must love his brother and sister also.

Before we were born again, we were the footstools of the world. We were trapped by the world's way of thinking and spent our lives loving and living in the sins of the world: the lust of the eyes, the lust of the flesh and the pride of life. We weren't overcomers; we were overcome by the anti-God system that has destroyed millions. This system is still destroying many spiritually retarded people every day.

Obedience by Faith

Faith is based on knowledge of God's Word and His character. The spirit of the world is in opposition to God. When we determine to stand in faith, the world loses its controlling influence over us. For example, the spirit of the world was drugs, women, and partying for me. But twenty-four years ago I gave my life to Christ and gave up my life of drugs, women, and partying. And when I gave my life to Christ, the influence of the world no longer had control of me. It could no longer come against me, because the power of God caused me to be an over-comer by the power of the Holy Spirit.

Because we are believers, men and women born of God we have overcome the world through our faith in Jesus Christ. It is being born of God and loving God and being obedient to His Word that puts us in position to be overcomers. The world has nothing on us any longer and nothing for us anymore. This is not something we could do on our own; we are overcomers because we are born again and dwell in Christ as Christ dwells in us. We have overcome the world's way of thinking. We have overcome the activities and the language of the world by our faith in Jesus the Messiah, Jesus the Christ. We may be in the world, but we're not of the world.

God's Blueprint

Chapter 24

THE CERTAINTY
OF GOD'S WITNESS

T his is He who came by water and blood
– Jesus Christ; not only by water, but by
water and blood. And it is the Spirit who
bears witness, because the Spirit is Truth.
> – First John 5:6 NKJV

This verse is refers to the baptism of Jesus Christ and
His death on the cross. The Holy Spirit bears witness
of this because the Holy Spirit is the Spirit of Truth.
He is the epitome of truth or *the foundation* of truth.
At the baptism of Jesus the Holy Spirit came down
from Heaven and lighted upon Him. There are three
that bear witness or agree to this; God the Father,
The Word (which is God the Son, Who was the re-
cipient of the power of God on Earth), and God the
Holy Spirit, Who executed the infilling of the Holy
Spirit on Jesus at His baptism. Then God the Father
declared the identity of Jesus, ***"This is My beloved
Son, in Whom I am well pleased." (See:*** Mt 3:17)

God's Blueprint

For there are three who bear witness; the Father, The Word, and the Holy Spirit; and these three are One. And there are three that bear witness on earth: the Spirit, the water and the blood; and these three agree as one. – 1 John 5:7-8

At His death, there are three that bear witness on the earth; The Holy Spirit, the water which came from His side mixed with blood that was shed on the cross. All of these actions are in agreement as one, because they are One.

The reason John taught this is because he was correcting a false teacher named Cerinthus, who claimed that the Spirit came on Jesus at His baptism, (which is true), but left before His death at the cross (which is not true). Jesus did not come to escape the cross but to embrace it. There are a number of people who still believe this today. The problem is it disagrees with the Bible; it disagrees with God's Word which has always been truth and always will be THE TRUTH. Whoever listens and believes any false prophet like Cerinthus will not have everlasting life because it does not agree with God's plan of salvation.

Note: The Holy Spirit came on Jesus when He was baptized by John the Baptist. God announced Him to whosoever that, *"This is My Son in Whom I am*

The Certainty of God's Witness

well pleased." At the death of Jesus, when He fulfilled the blueprint for man He cried out with a loud Voice saying *"Eli, Eli lama sabachthani!"* This translates, *"My God, My God, why have You forsaken Me?"* A little while later Jesus cried out again with a loud Voice and gave up His Spirit. His Spirit went back to God but His flesh was buried in the tomb until God raised Him from the dead.

> If we receive the witness of men, the witness of God is greater; for this is the witness of God which He testified of His Son. He who believes in the Son of God has the witness in himself; he who does believe God has made Him a liar, because he has not believed the testimony: that God has given us eternal life, and this life is in His Son. He who has the Son has life; he who does not have the Son of God does not have life. These things I have written to you who believe in the name of the Son of God, that you may know that you have eternal life, and that you may continue to believe in the name of the Son of God. – 1 John 5:9-13

If we receive the witness of men, there's a fifty-fifty chance the whole truth will not be told. There have been many false prophets whose given false witness like Cerinthus, Darwin, John Smith, and more recently Jim Jones, David Koresh, Tony Alamo, Charles

God's Blueprint

Manson, Yahweh Ben Yahweh, Deborah Green, Nx-ivn, Marshall Applewhite, Bagwan Shree Rajneesh, and a host of others who have been false witnesses and have been the source of many lost lives.

■ ■ ■

"He is the epitome of truth or the foundation of truth."

God's witness is greater than the witness of any man, or group of men or multitude of men and angels. God's witness is Whom He testified of—His Son Jesus the Christ. We must believe God and we must believe in God's testimony of Jesus, Who is the Christ. When we believe, we will have this witness within ourselves and we will know, that we know, that we know the pure unadulterated truth. We know God has given us His Son and through Him, we have eternal life because God says, *"He who has the Son, meaning Jesus the Christ, has life"* and he who does not believe, does not have life.

John wrote this particularly to believers in the Name of Jesus, the Son of God. He wanted to reiterate that believers have eternal life [now] and we must continue to believe in Jesus the Messiah; Jesus the Christ.

Chapter 25

CONFIDENCE AND COMPASSION IN PRAYER

Now this is the confidence that we have in Him, that if we ask anything according to His will, He hears us. And if we know that He hears us, whatever we ask, we know that we have the petitions that we have asked of Him. – First John 5:14 NKJV

One of the most wonderful, magnificent, and amazing benefits each believer possesses is the confidence that God hears our prayers. It's a beautiful thing. But our prayers must be according to *His will*. The Bible is His will, the doctrine of Jesus is His will, the obedience of the believers is His will and loving people is His will. The believers in Christ Jesus are confident that He hears our prayers, and we will receive whatever we ask. Isn't that awesome?

Believers of God have confidence of free access and *boldness* of speech in presenting their request to

Him. However, there is a limitation to the assurance that our prayers will be answered.

The assurance of asking in Jesus' Name:

> And whatever you ask in My name, that I will do, that My Father may be glorified in the Son. And if you ask anything in My Name, I will do it.
>
> – John 14:13

Whatever we ask in prayer in Jesus' Name will be done so that God the Father will be glorified in the Son. So when we pray, know that our prayers will be answered and know that answered prayer will glorify God the Son. Answered prayer is glorification of the Son and a witness to others.

> You didn't choose Me, but I chose you and appointed you that you should go and bear fruit, so that your fruit should remain, that whatever you ask the Father in My name He may give you.
>
> – John 15:16

I'm sure happy to be *chosen* on Jesus' team. A team where I could be useful in life, and I'm glad Christ chose me, because I didn't have enough spiritual sense to choose Him. I was so caught up in the world of sin, that I couldn't see the forest for the trees. Like

Confidence and Compassion...

many are doing in the world today, I thought I was having a good time: drinking, smoking and chasing women across the United States and Central America. But Christ chose me out of the world. In fact He chose me and appointed me that I should *bear fruit* or win souls for Him. So when I am bearing good fruit, I am setting myself up for answered prayer.

In fact, in the Book of Ephesians 1:3-4

> Blessed be the God and Father of our Lord Jesus Christ, who has blessed us with every spiritual blessing in the heavenly places in Christ, just as He chose us in Him before the foundation of the world, that we should be holy and without blame before Him in love.

We were on the mind of Christ before He shaped the world through the Voice of creation. In the mind of Christ, He knew that our lives will be a spectacle of sin. However He also knew us and chose us before there was any sin in the universe, (before the foundation of the world). He blessed us with every *spiritual blessing* in heavenly places in Christ Jesus and called us to be holy and without blame before Him in love.

Believers have an awesome life because our God is the _True_ and _Living_ God. *[emphasis mine]* Believers

231

God's Blueprint

in Christ Jesus are the only group of people in whom the Creator listens to our prayers and answers them according to the Word of God. All other religions do not have the comfort of a God Who listens and answers prayers—because their gods are dead. Every past leader of any type of cult, religious group, spiritualist faction or persuasion—is dead and can't answer any request from their followers. Allah can't answer prayer, Buddha cannot answer prayer, Hare Krishna cannot answer prayer, the god of the John Smith can't answer prayers and the Pope cannot answer our prayers. Every false or misguided religion around the world needs to pray for forgiveness for leading millions of people astray with their flesh driven religions; for the founders of every religion around the world are dead and stinking in their graves and can't answer anything, much less the prayers of their followers. In fact, all of these founders and followers of misguided and false religions will bow at the feet of Jesus. Jesus is the only one to die and rise out of the grave to sit at the right hand of God. He is alive and well and leads His Church on Earth and He is *the only One* Who answers our prayers. He may not answer when we want Him to answer, but He will eventually answer.

If anyone sees his brother sinning a sin that does not lead to death, he will ask, and He will give him life for those who commit sin not leading to

232

death. There is sin leading to death. I do not say that he should pray about that. All unrighteousness is sin, and there is sin not leading to death.

– 1 John 5:16-17

■ ■ ■

When we believe, we will have this witness within ourselves and we will know, that we know, that we know the pure unadulterated truth.

When we see a brother sinning that does not lead to death, we can ask God for forgiveness and God will grant him forgiveness. We should intercede for our fellow believers provided that we actually see a believer sinning and not hearing it through the grapevine. When I pastored a church in eastern Oklahoma and one of the brothers was accused of wrong doing, we would sit down and ask him the truth of the accusation because sometimes *Satan is the accuser of the brethren*. If the brother sinned we would pray for him, and continue our journey in the Kingdom of God There is sin that does not lead to death and we can have confidence that when we pray for a brother or sister in Christ that has sinned they will be forgiven. But there is a sin that will not be forgiven in this life or the next and that's blaspheming the Holy Spirit.

God's Blueprint

Therefore I say to you, every sin and blasphemy will be forgiven men, but the blasphemy against the Holy Spirit will not be forgiven. Anyone who speaks a word against the Son of Man, it will be forgiven them; but whosoever speaks against the Holy Spirit, it will not be forgiven him, either in this age or in the age to come. – Matthew 12:31-32

Back in the day, the Pharisees slandered the Holy Spirit by proficiently attributing the work of Jesus as the work of Satan when they said; "This fellow does not cast out demons except by Beelzebub, the ruler of the demons." (See: Mt 12:24) It was God working through Jesus when He healed the demon possessed man that was blind and mute. But the Pharisees' hearts were so hardened by their unbelief in Jesus they committed a crime against themselves and volunteered for eternal damnation. You can say anything you want about Jesus and if you want forgiveness, you will be forgiven; but if you say the devil is doing the good works through Jesus, you will find yourself extremely angry because your decision placed you in the Lake of Fire with a never ending discharge.

234

Chapter 26

KNOWING THE TRUTH – REJECTING THE FALSE

W e know that whoever is born of God does not sin; but he who has been born of God keeps himself, and the wicked one does not touch him. – First John 5:18 NKJV

We know! There are many Christians who do not have this mindset. Some people just don't believe they cannot live a life without sin. There are also preachers who preach that believers are going to sin. Most of these are stuck on the verse, "We have all sinned and have fallen short of the glory of God." (Romans 3:23) This is a true statement because God is Truth and His Bible declares it as truth. When you read this Scripture, you should notice that we have all sinned and we have all fallen short. Is this present tense or past tense? If this was present tense it would read we are still sinners and we are falling short of the glory of God. Instead it reads; we have all sinned! This statement is past tense and not present tense.

God's Blueprint

Before we were born again, we were falling into sin every day, several times a day. If we weren't stealing, we were lying, if we weren't getting high, we were scoping some male or female for sex, if we weren't gossiping we were robbing some establishment or somebody of their possessions. We were cheaters, drunks, and adulterers. We were lewd, idolatrous, haters, jealous and wrathful. We were full of selfish ambition and lived for *the love of money*. We were mean-spirited and had murderous hearts. The rewards for our deeds were leading us straight to Hell. Our wages of life were not glorious; but on the contrary, devastating and the only reward we had coming was to exist in the Lake of Fire with no parole, no discharge, no commutation, no escape and no way out. Everyone has sinned, practiced sin and lived exclusively in sin. But Jesus got off His throne in Heaven and came down to Earth and cleansed us from our sins. Those who wanted new lives, believed in Jesus, were baptized and were born again. Our sin nature became null and void and we were rewarded with a new nature, a godly nature in which God the Father, God the Son and God the Holy Spirit now dwell in us according to John 17. [Now] we are One in God the Father, One in God the Son and One in God the Holy Spirit. When we are born of God, our days of sin should be over because the Spirit of God dwells in us.

Knowing the Truth – Rejecting...

Before we were born again, the devil had hooks in our jaws leading us to this sin over here and that sin over there. But once we changed teams and chose Jesus, (actually He chose us before the foundation of the world), we now have the freedom to keep ourselves from sin and the devil for his demons have nothing on us and is not able to touch us. He will, however, verbally attempt to influence us back into the life of sin, but he will fall short in his endeavors.

> We know that we are of God, and the whole world lies under the sway of the wicked one.
> — 1 John 5:19

We know in our hearts that we are of God, our changed lives make it evident that we no longer belong to the world. We belong to God. The master of this world is the devil and he is *influencing* every one that is not born again to continue their lives in sin. In fact, he is encouraging the sinners of the world to step it up with their sin, to overdo in their sin, or go beyond the limits of normality. Thank God for saving us from our sins, and from this evil one, and dwelling in us by His Spirit.

And we know that the Son of God has come and has given us an understanding, that we may know Him who is true; and we are in Him who

God's Blueprint

is true, in His Son Jesus Christ. This is the true God and eternal life. – 1 John 5:20

When I was about ten years old, a heard my Pastor preach on the crucifixion of Jesus and that made me mad. The way the Romans beat Him, scourged Him and mocked Him really ticked me off. I wanted to get some M-16s and go back into time (like in the movies) and kill everyone who had something to do with the death of Jesus. Needless to say, I was spiritually misguided and didn't have a true spiritual understanding on why this was done to the Son of God. All I knew is that I wanted to kill them for killing Christ. But I'm okay now.

■ ■ ■

We know in our hearts that we are of God, our changed lives makes it evident that we no longer belong to the world. We belong to God.

We as a race of human beings were so far off the path of serving God that Jesus had to set us straight. Jesus did not come just to save us. He also came to the earth to give us understanding. He came to reveal The Father to us and taught us from the very mind, the very thoughts of God. He came to change us from a disorderly way of surviving to a godly order of living, praising, worshipping and faithfulness to the Almighty. He knew the devil was misleading people into false god worship, so He came to rescue us with THE TRUTH. Once we know the truth, we have the ability to recognize the truth and reject all false claims on living in the flesh and worshipping the devil in a life of sin.

Jesus came down, so that we may know the truth. Because the truth will always set us free. We, (as a people) had been living a lie until Jesus came and performed miracles that have never been performed before. Then He changed our sinful nature to a godly nature. Then He taught us Kingdom of God principals and characteristics starting with *the beatitudes*, the value of being *salt and light*, the importance of building your foundation on the teachings of Jesus, He taught us marriage and divorce, and oaths and loving our enemies. Jesus gave us a model prayer and taught us about fasting. He revealed the actions and the character of people in the last days. He taught us on the great rebellion from God's Word that has come to pass in this day. But most importantly, He taught us about how our relationship should be with God, Jesus and the Holy Spirit.

God's Blueprint

Chapter 27

IDOLS

Little children, keep yourselves from idols. Amen. – First John 5:21 NKJV

Through the years, men have craved, desired and longed for someone or something to worship; so they carved, whittled, shaped and fashioned materials of the earth and made them into idols to worship. There's something in every man and woman that wants to pay homage, respect, and reverence to something bigger than us. These feelings of reverence should be toward the True and Living God, but the flesh of men wants something they can see and touch. Men knew/know there's a true higher power (which is God Almighty), but yet, demons have influenced or stirred men to have the need to worship something fleshly. Romans one declares the understanding of God's invisible attributes being clearly seen by the things that are made, even His eternal power and Godhead, so people are without excuse, because although they knew God they did not glorify Him as God, nor were thankful, but became futile in their thoughts and their foolish hearts were darkened. So God let them be what they want to be.

> The idols of the nations are silver and gold, the works of men's hands. They have mouths, but they do not speak; Eyes they have, but they do not see; they have ears, but they do not hear. Nor is there any breath in their mouths. Those who make them are like them. So is everyone who trusts in them. – Psalm 135:15

There is an interesting story in 1 Samuel chapter 5 where the Philistines captured the Ark of the Covenant. The Philistines brought the Ark to their temple and placed it next to their ruling idol; Dagon. They went home and came back the next day and found that Dagon had fallen on his face in front of the Ark, as if he were bowing to the Ark of the Covenant. So they took Dagon and set him up again next to the Ark, and the next morning; again, they found their god face down before the Art of the Covenant. But this time Dagon's head and both of his palms were broken off.

Man set out and made gods, or something to worship with his hands. The men of the earth took the materials God created and prepared, and forged false idols to worship. The devil was and is clearly behind this *mindset,* from back in the garden until today. It is tru-

242

Idols

ly astounding that men will forsake God; yet, use the materials He created to craft, fashion, construct, and formulate an image to worship that has limitations in every way. These images have ears, but can't hear, they have eyes, but can't see, they have legs, but can't walk, and a head—without a brain. It is crazy to think these *manmade* images can help anyone sustain life.

■ ■ ■

Jesus came down so that we may know the truth. Because the truth will always set us free.

Men have to take care of their idols, their gods. They have to schedule maintenance on their gods and keep them clean. If an arm fell off their idol, they would have to repair it, and glue the idol's broken arm or leg back on. When something went wrong with their god they had to do whatever they could to fix it. They cannot comprehend the fact that false gods can't do anything for you—but lead you to Hell. And if you trust in these false gods you will be like them; spiritually blind, spiritually mute, spiritually dumb, spiritually retarded and spiritually paralyzed.

Idol worship is popular around the world. Sometimes movie stars are worshipped as gods. Michael

God's Blueprint

Jackson was one of the world's best entertainers and thousands upon thousands screamed his name as if he was a god. The Rolling Stones, The Beatles, Elvis, Prince and other popular singers, actors, sport stars, and rappers have been worshipped as 'a god' due to their God-given talents. In fact, celebrities with any standing are often worshipped for their craft instead of worshipping God, Who gave them the craft. These stars and superstars should be worshipping God instead of receiving worship and praise from the people of Earth.

Today, if we trust in our money instead of God, then our money is our god. If you spend all day on your Facebook, or YouTube, or any other social media page keeping up with the gossip, the rumors, and hearsay then that is your God. If you spend your days doing what you love to do without including God, Jesus and the Holy Spirit then you are serving gods that will not be able to help you on Judgment Day. There are television shows I don't dare to watch like *American Idol*. Just the name of that show gives me pause. There are other television shows, series and movies that are not hidden and are linked to the works of the devil as entertainment or the masses. If we are tuned in to shows like *Lucifer, Charmed, American gods*, horror shows and other shows portraying, witches, the occult, haunted houses and monsters from the underworld you're already serving gods, by giving them attention and your time instead of spending time with God. These anti-Christ based shows are developing the watcher into the world's way of thinking.

We need to take care of ourselves by understanding what we can do and what we shouldn't do. We should be busy in God's plans for us and the Body of Christ. We have come too far to sell out now, and the devil wants us badly. We must stay focused on Jesus and His ways until we die or the day He comes back for us.

[And He is coming back for us—very soon!]

About the Author (cont...)

... Pastor Mike has written and taught programs such as Christianity 101, Evidence of Salvation, and Growing in the Kingdom of God. He is also a four time published author of a series entitled The Kingdom of Light and Kingdom of Darkness, I, II, and III, and a verse by verse study of the Book of John.

Today, Pastor Hick is working as an Evangelist in the state of Oklahoma. He is also a volunteer in the state's prison system mainly at Davis Correctional Facility in Holdenville, Oklahoma.

Michael and his wife Sonja currently live in Oklahoma City and are parents of two children and four grandchildren.

For more information about Pastor Michael Ray Hicks and YAH Jireh Ministries go to our website:

www. yahjireh.org
or send email communications to:
mrhicks58@gmail.com

246

Enjoy these other great books from Bold Truth Publishing

Seemed Good to THE HOLY GHOST
by Daryl P Holloman

Effective Prison Ministries
by Wayne W. Sanders

TURN OFF THE STEW
by Judy Spencer

The Holy Spirit SPEAKS Expressly
by Elizabeth Pruitt Sloan

Matthew 4:4
Man shall not live by bread alone...
by Rick McKnight

VICTIM TO VICTOR (THE CHOICE IS YOURS)
by Rachel V. Jeffries

SPIRITUAL BIRTHING
Bringing God's Plans & Purposes into Manifestation
by Lynn Whitlock Jones

BECOMING PERFECT
Let The Perfector Perfect His Work In You
by Sally Stokes Weiesnbach

FIVE SMOOTH STONES
by Aaron Jones

Available at select bookstores and
www.BoldTruthPublishing.com